LOCOMOTION PAPERS — LP 111

THE BARNSTAPLE AND ILFRACOMBE RAILWAY

by
Colin G. Maggs

THE OAKWOOD PRESS

© Colin G. Maggs, 2021
First Edition 1978
Second Edition 1988
Third Edition 2021
Book redesigned using second edition text and new photographs added.

ISBN 978-0-85361-761-7

Printed by
P2D Books, 1 Newlands Rd, Westoning, Bedford, MK45 5LD

'N' class 2-6-0 No. 31841 crosses the Taw estuary between Barnstaple Town and Junction stations, 1st August, 1952. Although the engine is in a livery of black lined with a BR crest, it carries the Southern Railways version of the BR number on its buffer beam.

R.E. Toop

Acknowledgements

Grateful acknowledgement for assistance is due to: H.V. Barley; H.J. Brian; Mrs H.S. Chugg; Devon Record Office; I. Dinmore; S. Hatchley; J.J. Herd; J. Longhurst; Ilfracombe Museum; R.A. Lumber; G.A. Morris, North Devon Athenaeum; G. Pothecary; Public Record Office; C.F. Roberts; R.J. Sellick; K.G. Smith and D.R. Steggles, Devon County Library.

Special thanks must go to V. Thompson who checked the manuscript, P.K. Tunks who helped with information regarding train services and J. Lock who carried out part of the initial research.

Published by
The Oakwood Press, 54-58 Mill Square, Catrine, KA5 6RD
Telephone: 01290 551122   Website: www.stenlake.co.uk

Contents

	Introduction	5
One	Early Railway Schemes	7
Two	The Line Opens	31
Three	Description of the Line	37
Four	The Great Western Loop	67
Five	Locomotives	69
Six	Rolling Stock	81
Seven	Permenant Way and Signalling	83
Eight	Pasenger and Freight Services	87
Nine	Prestige Trains	105
Ten	Accidents	117
Eleven	Closure	121

Appendices

One	LSWR Working Timetable August 1874	125
Two	Speed Limits	126
Three	Atlantic Coast Express Timings: 1936	127
Four	Train Logs: 1932 and 1933	128
Five	Instructions affecting Western Region Staff when working over the SR: October 1960	130
Six	Station Statistics	132

Bibliography		134
Index		135

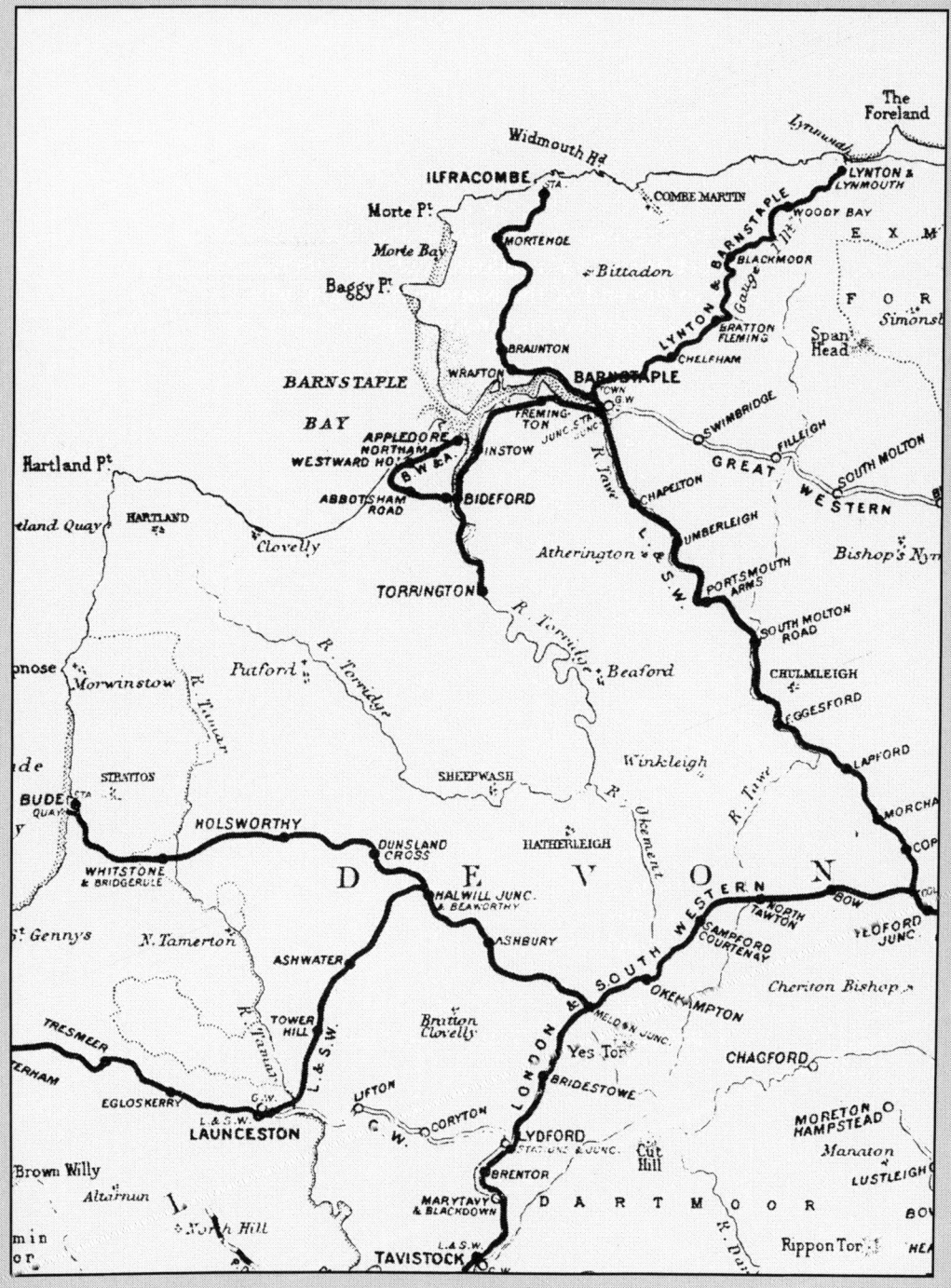

1910 Railway Clearing House Map of the area and its railways.

Introduction

Ilfracombe is a town with a history. Known in Saxon times as Alfreincombe, it consisted of a few dwellings by the harbour, which is one of the few natural havens along that coast giving shelter from the prevailing winds. In 1346 the town provided Edward III with six ships and 96 seamen to' help fight the war against France. Over the ensuing centuries, the town declined as Barnstaple and Bideford, having larger anchorages and better communications, took over its trade. Its decline continued down to the end of the Napoleonic Wars, when it began to change from a market town and fishing port into a watering place. In the eighteen-twenties Ilfracombe was frequented for bathing and made "an agreeable summer residence". When the town deliberately set out to attract visitors in the eighteen-thirties, population grew rapidly, but its fastest growth was between 1861 and 1891 when the population doubled from 3851 to 7692 and then remained nearly static a contrast to the continuously growing resorts of South Devon. In 1895, Murray's *A Handbook for Travellers in Devon and Cornwall* complained of Ilfracombe that "the railway from Barnstaple has given increased facility for reaching it; and those who desire quiet and comparative solitude will do better to pitch their tents at Westward Ho or Lynton".

Until the coming of the railway, access to Ilfracombe was either by road with considerable gradients to surmount, or by water. Steamer services were run from various ports in the British Channel; from Bristol the trip took seven hours. Due to the lack of a commercial hinterland, coupled with the seasonal nature of the traffic, steamer services to Ilfracombe tended to be haphazard. The Great Western Railway, Midland Railway, Bristol & Exeter Railway and Bristol & Portishead Railway, operated through bookings in conjunction with the Portishead Steam Ship Company, from their stations to Ilfracombe, passengers having a choice of sailing from the Cumberland Basin, Bristol and enjoying a trip through the Avon Gorge, or travelling on by rail and boarding the ship at Portishead Pier. Within four years of the railway's arrival at Ilfracombe, steamship services had dwindled until there was only Pockett's packet from Swansea and the GWR service from Portishead, the latter ceasing in 1884.

Advert from *The Official Guide to the Midland Railway,* published 1893.

LONDON AND SOUTH WESTERN RAILWAY,

THE SHORTEST, QUICKEST, AND MOST DIRECT ROUTE BETWEEN LONDON AND THE WEST OF ENGLAND.

THE PARADE, ILFRACOMBE.
(From a photograph by Mr. J. C. Catford, Ilfracombe.)

THIS popular railway runs through the most beautiful scenery in North and South Devon, skirts the south-western coast, and owns communication with the Isle of Wight, *via* Portsmouth Harbour, *via* Stokes Bay, *via* Southampton, and *via* Lymington. It also supplies frequent services between London and the Thames Valley. Passengers travelling by the London and South Western expresses may at Exeter make connections for Torquay, Dartmouth, and South Devon; while at Plymouth similar connections can be made for Falmouth, Penzance, and South Cornwall. Pullman Cars run in the principal trains between London and Brockenhurst (for the New Forest) and Bournemouth.

THE INVALID'S WALK, BOURNEMOUTH.
(From a photograph by Messrs. Miell & Ridley, Bournemouth.)

EXPRESS TRAINS BETWEEN LONDON

(Waterloo Station),

AND

EXETER IN $3\frac{3}{4}$ HOURS.
PLYMOUTH IN $5\frac{1}{4}$ HOURS.
BROCKENHURST (FOR NEW FOREST) IN 2 HRS.
PORTSMOUTH IN 2 HOURS.
ILFRACOMBE IN 6 HOURS.
SWANACE IN $3\frac{3}{4}$ HOURS.
WEYMOUTH IN $3\frac{3}{4}$ HOURS.
RYDE IN $2\frac{2}{3}$ HOURS.
LYNTON IN $8\frac{1}{2}$ HOURS.
BOURNEMOUTH IN $2\frac{1}{2}$ HOURS
SOUTHAMPTON IN $1\frac{3}{4}$ HOURS.
VENTNOR IN $3\frac{1}{2}$ HOURS.

For full particulars, conditions, and tourists' fares, see South Western Railway time-table books and tourist programmes.

Chapter One

Early Railway Schemes

The earliest proposal for a rail link between Barnstaple and Ilfracombe was the London to Salisbury and Exeter Railway surveyed by Charles Dean of Exeter in the early eighteen-forties under the direction of J. Herapath and Colonel Landmann, RE. The undated map of the scheme showed an extension from Exeter through Crediton and Barnstaple to Ilfracombe which was marked as a "proposed Irish Packet Station", but the scheme proved to be abortive. 1845, the year of the Railway Mania, brought forth an ambitious plan entitled "The Great West of England Railway" for a line from Basingstoke to Falmouth with branches to Torquay and Ilfracombe, but this proposal was equally unsuccessful.

The opening of the North Devon Railway & Docks Company (NDR) from Crediton to Barnstaple on 1st August, 1854 allowed through running from Exeter. This single broad gauge line was worked by the Bristol & Exeter Railway (B&E) until 28th July, 1855, when it was taken over by Thomas Brassey the contractor who built it. On 1st January, 1863 the lease was taken over by the London & South Western Railway (LSWR), the gauge being mixed from 1st March, 1863; the LSWR purchased the line outright on 1st January, 1865.

With the service to Barnstaple an accomplished fact, an Exeter solicitor, Robert Wreford, began developing his plan for extending the

The arrival at Barnstaple of the first train on the North Devon Railway, 12th July, 1854. Notice the grandstand on the far right. *Author's collection*

Triumphal arch on Barnstaple Bridge celebrating the opening of the North Devon Railway 12th July, 1854.
Author's collection

TRIUMPHAL ARCH, BARNSTAPLE-BRIDGE.

railway to Ilfracombe, by now a recognized resort and in need of railway communication with the rest of the country. From 1854 Wreford was in constant contact with the three railways interested in North Devon – the LSWR, the North Devon and the Bristol & Exeter, spending a considerable sum on the project.

In the late eighteen-fifties at a public meeting in Ilfracombe, Thomas Brassey who was working the North Devon line, offered to construct a railway to the town on condition that it was unopposed. This type of condition was typical of Brassey, who was against long-drawn-out arguments, but his plans came to nothing apart from arousing the interest of the Rev. Benjamin Price, an interesting character, formerly the incumbent of Christ Church, Ilfracombe, later minister of the Free Church in the town, and afterwards Bishop Primus of the Free Church of England. Price was associated with Wreford and later, as Chairman of the local committee, remained in control of affairs at the Ilfracombe end from February 1861 until the passing of the Act. On through traffic,

Wreford hoped to obtain a rebate of £2000 per annum jointly from the LSWR and North Devon Railway, and in addition £500 from the B&E. Wreford was on good terms with Bircham & Co., the LSWR's solicitors; J.E. Errington, Consulting Engineer to the LSWR; and Thomas Brassey, the contractor. Captain Charles E. Mangles, Chairman of the LSWR, and William Tite, Chairman of the North Devon, both visited Ilfracombe and were in favour of a line. In October 1860 the LSWR promised to subscribe over ten years £10,000 towards a standard gauge line should the North Devon do likewise and the B&E subscribed £5,000, but nothing came of the proposal.

The main problem was to find a good route to Ilfracombe, a difficult task as a range of hills some 800 feet above sea level stretched across the path only three miles south of the town. Two schemes were proposed. The eastern, or Bittadon, route left Barnstaple and ran almost due north through Bittadon, crossing the hills at a height of about 800 feet before entering Ilfracombe from the east and terminating above the harbour. The western, or Braunton, route ran north-west from Barnstaple down the right bank of the River Taw before turning inland to run through Braunton, then crossing the hills at a lower level than the eastern route to terminate above the town.

Errington and his assistant, W.R. Galbraith, went over the ground and selected the western route, the eastern being too expensive to adopt. The greatest opposition to the western route came from Sir William Williams, owner of Heanton Court near Wrafton, who for the next ten years was against a railway near his house, for the proposed Braunton route ran between Heanton Court and the river.

Williams, whose main residence was at Tregullow, Cornwall, owned 3,000 acres at Heanton. The last resident owner of the Court died back in 1801 and since then part of the house had been pulled down, many of the windows built up, the park timber cut and the deer destroyed. The *North Devon Journal* pointed out that his grievance of injury to the "mansion house of Heanton Court" by cutting off its river frontage could hardly be sustained as "persons unacquainted with the locality will scarcely conceive that the unsightly heap of irregular and dilapidated buildings situated near the three mile post on the road to Braunton is dignified by the high-sounding title of 'mansion house'. The removal of the entire structure would rid the landscape of a blot and the public an eyesore, which most certainly ought not to stand in the way of a railway through an important district."

Williams had conferred benefits on the district by spending vast sums on enclosing and draining a large area covered by the sea and thus adding hundreds of acres to that fertile valley. Williams probably adopted his anti-railway stance holding the narrow view that as he had reclaimed the land for farming, it should be used for no other purpose, not appreciating that a railway would bring further prosperity to the land. Despite Williams's attitude, the main cause of failure in 1860 was the apathy of the people of Ilfracombe and lack of confidence in Wreford, who had deposited plans for the line, but was unable to form a directorate, and so no application could be made to Parliament.

Wreford's failure was connected with the promotion of the Exmouth Railway in south-east Devon, authorised as a broad gauge line in 1855. He was the company's solicitor, but acquisition of shares by standard gauge interests, with the idea of a connection with the sanctioned extension of the LSWR to Exeter, conflicted with the broad gauge ideas, and after an exchange of opinions, the line was constructed to standard gauge. Wreford was dismissed and alleged that this was to make way for a nominee of the standard gauge party. Through this action Wreford sustained a serious financial loss, his reputation as a railway promoter also suffering.

Early in 1861 attempts were made to remedy the faults of the previous year, and the Rev. Price, supported by the Chairman of the LSWR and the North Devon, was appointed Chairman of the local committee set up to overcome the prejudice against Wreford. The LSWR's solicitors at first gave procedural advice (unofficially), but later they became actively associated with the promoters as their solicitors, especially Frederick Bircham himself who was sincere and hard-working in his attempts to promote the Ilfracombe Railway.

A meeting was held to decide on the best route, the following being unanimously adopted. The line was to leave the North Devon at Bishops Tawton about a mile south of Barnstaple station and later known as Barnstaple Junction, then skirting the town to the east, run to Braunton and the Foxhunters Inn, climbing the valley leading to Trimstone and tunnelling into the Folly and Slade Valleys to a terminus at Higher Horne, Ilfracombe. An extension was to lead through another tunnel at the back of the town and run to the harbour. This route differed from the western one of the previous year in that it tunnelled through the range of hills and avoided a long detour to the west from Foxhunters Inn, thereby saving two miles.

When Galbraith had finished the survey, application was made to the LSWR for support in carrying the Bill through Parliament and also for the assistance necessary to enable a contract for the construction of the line to be placed. Unfortunately for the Ilfracombe Railway, the LSWR was in the middle of negotiations with the North Devon Railway (NDR) for the purchase or leasing of that line, and so was therefore unwilling to take on more liabilities at Barnstaple until its position there was known. But nevertheless, the LSWR's reply was encouraging and left the applicants hopeful of success the following year.

Towards the end of 1861 another group of engineers arrived at Ilfracombe, associated with a scheme for a line called the Devon & Somerset Railway (D&S), to run from Taunton to Barnstaple with an extension to Ilfracombe. Interested parties at Ilfracombe wisely foresaw the delay and expense a rival scheme could cause, and sent letters to the LSWR and NDR companies urging them to secure the area, but they seem to have had little effect and the warning went largely unheeded.

Early in 1862 Wreford suggested that immediate arrangements should be made with the landowners, but the committee, in view of a pledge given to Sir William Williams the previous year, deferred any meeting of the landowners until the impracticability of any other route could be shown. Meanwhile attempts were made to gain the support of Barnstaple.

In July an agreement was reached whereby the LSWR would lease the NDR from 1st January, 1863. This meant that the standard gauge could be laid into Barnstaple and that the LSWR Board was now in a position to entertain proposals for an Ilfracombe extension, these being put by a deputation which visited Waterloo. With an idea of easing the steep gradients and sharp curves of the western route, in September the LSWR Board sent Galbraith, who had succeeded the late Errington as Consultant Engineer, to survey the eastern route through Bittadon and Berrynarbor. In his report he estimated the cost of the line which included five tunnels, several viaducts, a lofty embankment and heavy cuttings, to be in the region of £220,000 compared with the estimated £160,000 for the western route and an additional £20,000 if the harbour branch was included. Galbraith reported that he considered the extra cost was too much to pay for the easier gradients obtained by the heavy engineering works on the eastern route and so recommended the Board to adopt the western route. The LSWR then advised its shareholders to sanction an arrangement whereby the company was to work the Ilfracombe line for 45 per cent of the gross receipts; to pay a rebate of £2000 which was to be continued only so long as that, or a lesser amount, was required to pay a dividend of 4½ per cent, and to have the option of purchase on terms securing 4½ per cent to the Ilfracombe shareholders.

In January 1863 the necessary deposit was made in Chancery. The

Ilfracombe Railway Bill proposed raising a capital of £180,000 in £20 shares with additional borrowing powers of £60,000. The first Directors were Joshua Avery, Richard Huxtable, William Huxtable, the Rev. Benjamin Price and William Stanney Toms, Messrs Bircham & Co. and Robert Wreford being the joint solicitors. The proposed route was the western one from a junction with the NDR at Bishops Tawton, tunnelling through the hills and making a final descent of 1 in 33 for 1 mile 7 furlongs to a terminus at Ilfracombe, near the old Barnstaple Road and 160 ft above sea level, the line having a total length of 14 miles 75 chains.

In Parliament the Bill was supported by the LSWR, NDR and the B&E. Thomas E. Harrison, Engineer-in-Chief of the North Eastern Railway, recommended the western line, but this route was opposed by Sir William Williams. Mr Whitley (Williams's agent) put forward plans for an eastern route and was backed by the Great Western's Consulting Engineer John Fowler, who did not come in his official capacity, but stated that a gradient of 1 in 33 was inconsistent with safety. The eastern line had a ruling gradient of 1 in 40 compared with 1 in 33 and only one curve of 20 chains radius instead of eight. The gradients of the western line were expected to involve greater working expenses than the other route, while at Ilfracombe the western line station would have been 160 ft above sea level compared with the eastern 145 ft. Fowler said that the estimated cost was £173,799 12s. 9d. for the western line and £166,673 3s. 0d. for the eastern line. With the weight of this evidence, the Lords Committee felt obliged to throw out the Bill.

When the news of the Bill's failure reached Braunton and Ilfracombe on Saturday 25th April, bitter disappointment was expressed. At Braunton some of the inhabitants expressed their dislike of Whitley (who through pressing for an eastern route had robbed Braunton of its railway) and formed a procession which perambulated round the town with banners and brass band escorting an effigy of him drawn by two donkeys. Whitley managed to capture this figure, probably hoping to ascertain from the clothing who were the perpetrators; it was humorously suggested by Wreford that he should be prosecuted for theft. Whitley's detractors ultimately regained its possession, hung the effigy on a gallows and then burnt it to ashes.

At Ilfracombe even more violent scenes took place. As the omnibus from Barnstaple with the promoters arrived in the town at 10.00 pm, a crowd of two or three hundred started a riot. W.S. Toms was carried shoulder high to his home and then the crowd, increasing to seven or eight hundred by 11.30 pm, attacked with brickbats and missiles, the homes of George Carter and R.H. Moon, two of Williams's supporters. Eighteen panes of glass were broken in Carter's house and nine in Moon's shop, and it was fortunate that Carter's shop windows were shuttered or even greater damage would have been inflicted. At 2.00 am on Sunday morning the Riot Act was read by Captain Vye, the resident magistrate, but the crowd did not disperse until 4.00 am.

On 27th April an open air public meeting attended by 2000 people was held in the High Street opposite the Town Hall to censure Carter and Moon. When Carter returned from London on 28th April, he received a shower of rotten eggs (despite police protection) from Ilfracombe ladies. Two days later, when he bravely ventured out, they forced him to an undignified run for shelter in a shop. The townspeople were still not satisfied, and on 4th May effigies of the pair were paraded and a gallows erected for their public execution.

The excitement of the riot had scarcely died down when a plan for the Devon & Somerset Railway appeared in the autumn. This caused a considerable amount of discussion and· ill-feeling between the various parties. In November a private meeting for supporters was held at Ilfracombe. It was not a very enthusiastic gathering and the only outcome being to recommend the people of Ilfracombe not to commit themselves until both schemes had had a fair hearing; but within a few days it was announced that they had decided in favour of the D&S proposal. Meanwhile, throughout the summer, negotiations had been proceeding with the LSWR, and in June 1863 an LSWR express carried boards labelled "Exeter and Ilfracombe" – though not revealing that the Barnstaple to Ilfracombe section had to be by road.

In September 1863 the LSWR Directors advised the promoters to make another application to Parliament in the next Session, and although the Board believed the western route to be the best, suggested that the eastern route be adopted to avoid the opposition of Sir William Williams and the possibility of the D&S also applying for a line to Ilfracombe. When Galbraith surveyed the route he found it could not be built for less than £210,000 against the £166,673 suggested by Fowler. Galbraith's figures were supported by tenders put in for the construction of the line: Messrs Robert Sharp £212,000; Messrs Brassey £213,000 and Messrs Waring £220,000. The scheme involved two tunnels, two viaducts (one of which was 168 ft in height) and a descent of 3¼ miles on a gradient of 1 in 40 to a terminus at Ilfracombe, 150 ft above the harbour, to which a 54¼ ch. tramway was to run on a gradient of 1 in 8.5. The length of the proposed line was 12 miles 29¼ chains.

14   THE BARNSTAPLE AND ILFRACOMBE RAILWAY

The broad guage 2-4-0 *Creedy* at Barnstaple. Its name appears on both the boiler and the tender.
Author's collection

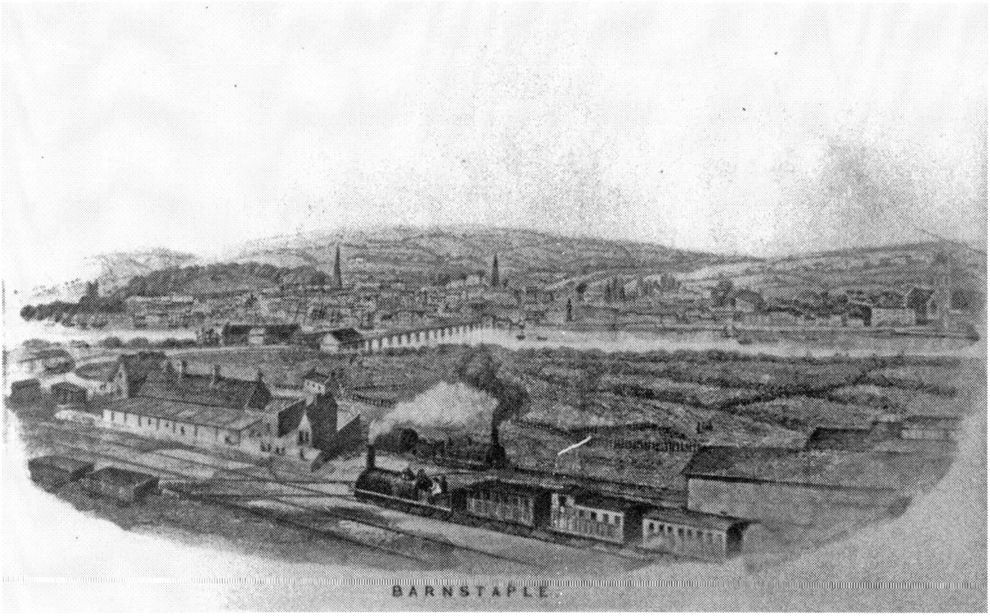

A broad gauge train arrives at Barnstaple station in 1853. The goods shed can be seen on the right whilst in the middle distance can be seen the multi-arched Long Bridge crossing the River Taw.   *Author's collection*

The LSWR agreed to subscribe £50,000 in deferred shares not entitled to dividend until 4½ per cent had been paid on the ordinary shares, the LSWR having powers to provide a further £60,000. It was also to have powers to lease the line at a rental of 55 per cent of the gross receipts and be able to appoint three of the six Directors and to have the option of purchase securing 4½ per cent to the Ilfracombe company shareholders. The LSWR named Ralph Heneage Dutton, Edward John Hutchins and Charles Edward Mangles as its Directors on the Board, the other three being William Huxtable, Benjamin Price and William Stanney Toms.

Opposition to the LSWR scheme occurred in January 1864 when the D&S introduced its Bill. The Act for a line from Taunton to Barnstaple was passed on 29th July, 1864, *27 & 28 Vic. cap 307,* but its extension to Ilfracombe had been rejected by the House of Lords on 15th March, 1864. This news was received with much jubilation at Ilfracombe, the majority of the townspeople remaining loyal to the Ilfracombe Railway (IR), the local company.

The IR bill was in the committee stage on 2nd June, 1864. There were three petitions against it: from the D&S, the Ilfracombe Harbour Company (which was connected with the D&S) and the landowners. Although the D&S did not attend Parliament to support its petition, the committee insisted that a clause be inserted making the IR build all overbridges and tunnels to a sufficient width to take a single line of mixed gauge track, so with this amendment and another shortening the harbour branch to 2 furlongs in length, the Bill passed the committee stage on 6th June, 1864. The LSWR naturally objected to the mixed gauge clause and at first declined to accept the amendment, but after the people of Ilfracombe had unsuccessfully petitioned Parliament that the Bill might pass without this clause, an arrangement was made whereby the D&S were admitted to joint ownership, the D&S replacing the private subscribers to the IR. The Act, *27 & 28 Vic. cap 272,* was passed on 25th July, 1864 and authorised a capital of £210,000 and borrowing powers of £70,000. Little did the LSWR know what trouble it was letting itself in for when it reluctantly acquiesced.

An Agreement was scheduled to the Act making provision that the D&S should declare its option to become joint owners of the Ilfracombe line with the LSWR on or before 10th October, 1864 so that the necessary powers could be sought in the 1865 session. The notice was duly given by the D&S.

Early in November 1864 Robert Wreford suddenly died, his death coming as a great shock to his friends at Ilfracombe. It was believed that the trouble he experienced with the Exmouth Railway and his numerous attempts to obtain redress on the matter, contributed to his demise. His efforts in getting the railway to Ilfracombe were not forgotten, and at the procession to the ceremony of cutting the first sod, his portrait formed a prominent feature.

The first meeting of the directors of the IR took place at Waterloo station on 20th October, 1864. Captain Mangles (Chairman of the LSWR) was elected Chairman, and Frederick Clarke (Secretary of the LSWR) was elected Secretary. On 2nd February, 1865 the LSWR Board agreed to ask Galbraith to proceed with a permanent survey of the line, he being appointed Engineering Superintendent for £320 per mile. This payment included the enlarged working survey, staking out the line, preparation of all plans and drawings and the superintendence of construction, the station buildings alone being excepted. The D&S plan to purchase Ilfracombe Harbour was not proceeded with. The same month the IR, jointly with the LSWR, deposited petitions in Parliament against measures being promoted by the D&S: the proposed D&S junction line at Barnstaple with the North Devon line and the abandonment of a portion of the IR, the LSWR reacting very strongly against the suggestion, as the scheme would have taken land required for the IR. The LSWR also opposed the D&S Bill for effecting joint purchase with the LSWR of the IR as the clauses were so framed that the D&S was not required to carry much pecuniary responsibility.

An Act, *28 Vic. cap 71*, ratifying the arrangements by the LSWR and D&S was obtained on 2nd June, 1865 and led to Ilfracombe having its railway without needing to subscribe to it, and not only that, the line was to be of mixed gauge and connected to both the LSWR and Bristol & Exeter Railways, giving the townspeople the advantage of alternative routes. Up to 31st December, 1864, 2700 shares had been bought by the LSWR and only 77 by others. In July 1865 the LSWR took a further 2473 shares making an aggregate total of 5250 shares at £20 each, or £105,000 nominal capital. The D&S received a call of £2 a share on its 5250 shares. On 1st August, John McMillan, the D&S Secretary, wrote saying that the matter was receiving attention, but failed to back it up with cash. In spite of several reminders from the IR, the D&S made no further communication, the truth being that, because of the poor state of the money market, it lacked funds to buy the shares and in November the IR took legal proceedings against the company. Meanwhile Galbraith had staked out the line and prepared a working plan and section, but in November the question of letting contracts for building the line had to be adjourned pending the unsatisfactory state of relations with the D&S. On 18th January, 1866 a further call of £2 a share was made.

The attitude of the LSWR at this time was indicated by Archibald Scott, the traffic manager who wrote: "We are ready to begin and have paid up all our calls, and obtained judgment against the Devon and Somerset for the calls due by that company, and unless some satisfactory arrangement be made we shall enforce that judgment. We would prefer to go on pleasantly with them rather than be forced to coerce them, and I am in hopes that some settlement may now be come to enabling the Railway to be commenced in earnest."

In October 1866 the IR solicitor said that he was authorised under the Judgments obtained against the D&S to serve notices on D&S shareholders to the effect that the IR meant to apply for execution against each shareholder for the non-payment of calls under the thirty sixth clause of the Companies Clauses Consolidation Act of 1845. This had the effect of making three D&S shareholders forward cheques to the IR. The IR solicitor adopted the sensible scheme of proceeding with only a few of the cases in which the amounts were rather large, allowing the

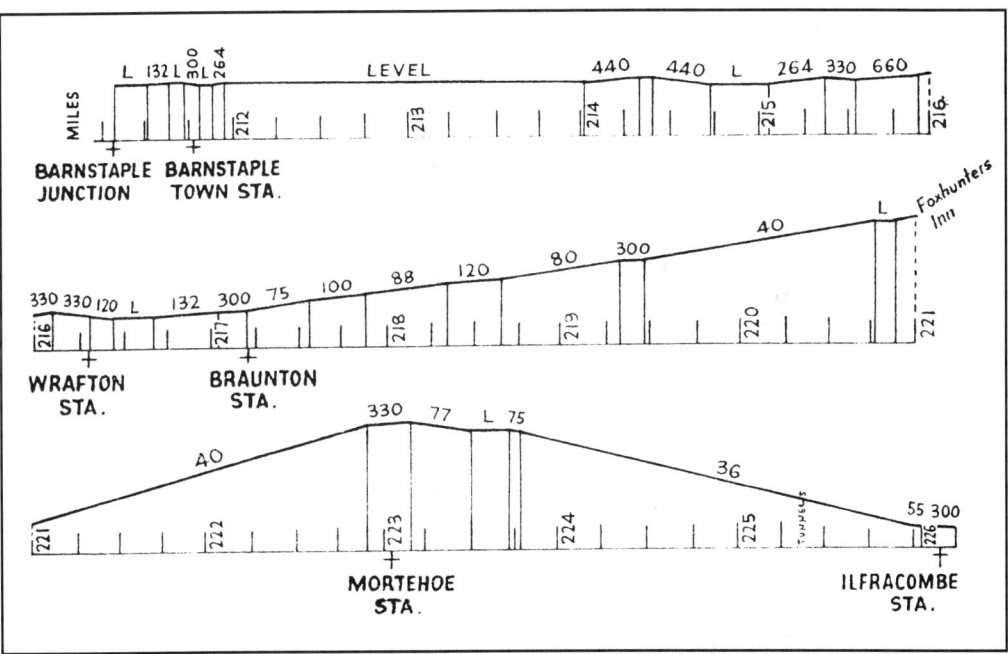

Gradient profile of the line.

rest to stand over for a time. In December- 1866 Messrs Pickering, contractors for the Devon & Somerset's Taunton to Barnstaple line, fearing non-payment, asked the Court to restrain the IR from further action under the orders obtained against the D&S in reference to the unpaid calls. This resulted in Vice Chancellor Stuart granting an injunction restraining the IR from any further action in the various proceedings taken against the D&S shareholders and for obtaining possession of their lands. The IR solicitor was instructed to appeal against this injunction; the Lords Justices wholly and without reserve, reversed the Vice Chancellor's decision, so the IR was free to prosecute certain shareholders and in March 1867 writs were issued against more D&S shareholders. The D&S proposed withdrawing from partnership with the IR and desired the repeal of the IR Act of 1865, but the latter company declined.

The D&S proposed indemnifying the IR against the forfeiture of the Parliamentary deposit of £16,800 made in respect of the IR Act of 1864 in case the D&S Bill for repealing the IR Act 1865 received the sanction of Parliament in the next session. The B&E withdrew its Bill for purchasing the D&S as it had no wish to be liable for the payment of the IR shares. An IR Bill of 1867 for extra time for construction was withdrawn, and on 12th August, 1867, under *30 and 31 Vic. cap 172*, the D&S received powers to shed its IR commitments on the grounds of inability to construct its line from Taunton to Barnstaple and of still greater inability to provide its share of money for the Ilfracombe line. The D&S was required to meet half the IR expenses, including the 1863 Bill, and could only leave the shareholders' register by making payment within three months of its IR debts, but as no payment was made, the 1867 Act became abortive.

This forced the IR to seek an abandonment Act of 25th June, 1868, *31 & 32 Vic. cap 171*, which required the discharge of all its debts before its dissolution. Anxious to bring its affairs to an end so that a fresh start could be made, the IR tried writs of *fiere facias* (the process of executing a judgment) against the D&S shareholders. On 9th November, 1877 judgment for £11,492 4s. 0d. and costs was obtained against the D&S, but this remained largely unpaid, with interest accruing at 4 per cent. When the Great Western Railway bought the D&S on 1st July, 1901, it agreed to pay the LSWR £1500 in cash and £1570 nominal value in GWR 2½ per cent debentures in exchange for £12,566 D&S debentures, this allowing the dissolution of the IR on 21st November, 1901.

Returning to August 1867, it was reported that month that although the IR was as yet unmade, its cost to date had been £46,370 9s. 4d. On 7th

November, 1867 the IR solicitor was instructed to wind up the affairs of the company. Galbraith agreed to the reduction of his fees of £4080 to £1700, since he had not superintended the actual building of the line.

In October 1868 the IR received a letter from the LSWR suggesting that under Section V of the Regulation of Railways Act, *31 & 32, Vic. cap 119* passed on 31st July that year, a light railway might be constructed between Barnstaple and Ilfracombe. Negotiations were once again resumed and in response to the promoters, Galbraith once more surveyed the line, finding the western route the best and only practicable one for a light railway. A suggestion that the River Taw could be bridged lower down at Fremington, thereby avoiding Sir William Williams's property, was rejected as this would have obstructed shipping going to Barnstaple. It was found impossible to apply to Parliament in the 1869 session, but plans were kept before the public eye.

At a public meeting held in February 1869 to consider the formation of a company, a novel scheme was put forward by Messrs Lucas and Wilkinson, the plan being to tunnel under the Taw between Fremington and Braunton where the river at its narrowest was rather more than a quarter of a mile wide. The line was then to cross the range of hills using J.B. Fell's centre-rail adhesion system, then currently in operation over the Mont Cenis Pass, and go through West Down, Trimstone and Twitchen to finish at a terminus near Ilfracombe Church. This line was to have been 9½ miles in length and its cost £83,000.

The Rev. Price then announced that a scheme under the auspices of the LSWR would soon be put before the town, so a committee was formed to look at any scheme which might be brought forward. Early in 1870 two such schemes were considered: an eastern scheme with a proposed capital of £120,000 and borrowing powers of £40,000 and a western, with a proposed capital of £150,000 and borrowing powers of £35,000. Both schemes were put to Barnstaple Town Council on 10th January, 1870. Galbraith spoke for the western route, the press reporting that

> ... the line by the Braunton route was not only the best for the county generally, but the best for Ilfracombe itself inasmuch as the gradients were the most easy, and a larger population would be served. There has always been some difficulty in passing the town of Barnstaple. On the one hand they might proceed from the present LSWR station, and cross the river at Pottington, and thus wholly avoid the town property; another way was to branch off at Pill Bridge, and pass around the town without crossing the river at all; but there seemed to him to be considerable disadvantages in going by that route,

inasmuch as it would be necessary to make a circuit of the town and interfere with every road in the parish of Barnstaple, besides destroying a good deal of property. There was also the objection that they would have no direct access by this route to the LSWR station, which would be a source of great inconvenience. His own views were in favour of crossing the river by a bridge at Pottington, but he was given to understand that there would be a very strong feeling on the part of the inhabitants against such a procedure on the grounds that it would interfere with navigation of the river.

Gould, the borough surveyor, suggested "that the river should be crossed immediately below the present bridge and acting on this suggestion Mr Galbraith had laid out the plans that had been deposited." Galbraith said, "A further examination of the country has enabled us to do something more than had been done before, namely to get down to Ilfracombe with a gradient of 1 in 37 instead of 1 in 33, which is the gradient at present worked without any trouble or inconvenience between the St David's and Queen Street stations at Exeter." (Actually the gradient St David's to Queen Street was 1 in 37.)

The advantages of this line were that a siding 150 ft in length was to be laid on the quay at Barnstaple for direct loading, and the station placed near the foot of Cross Street. The Railway company was to give Barnstaple 195 ft of additional quay accommodation and deepen the water by 2 ft. The existing quay walls were in a dilapidated condition and would soon have required rebuilding, so the town council was saved this outlay.

Jenkins, the Engineer for the eastern scheme, claimed that it was the shortest and cheapest line and the best adapted to supply the needs of the district; that it was the most convenient for the town of Barnstaple and would give the least interference with river navigation. "It was proposed that the station would be at the top of Bear Street, just opposite the entrance to Fort Hill fields. This was in his opinion the most convenient place in which they could make a station for Barnstaple, being in such close proximity to the corn exchange and market, and the principal parts of the town."

On being put to the vote, twelve were for the western scheme, one for the eastern and four abstained. On 18th January, 1870 it was announced that the eastern line promoters were withdrawing their Bill after having their scheme rejected at Barnstaple and Ilfracombe. Meanwhile the LSWR established a foot in the door at Ilfracombe by announcing that the company intended opening an office in the town where passengers and goods could be booked by coach to Barnstaple, or through to any station on the LSWR. Early in 1870 the LSWR

EARLY RAILWAY SCHEMES

Barnstaple in broad gauge days, 1853.   *Author's collection*

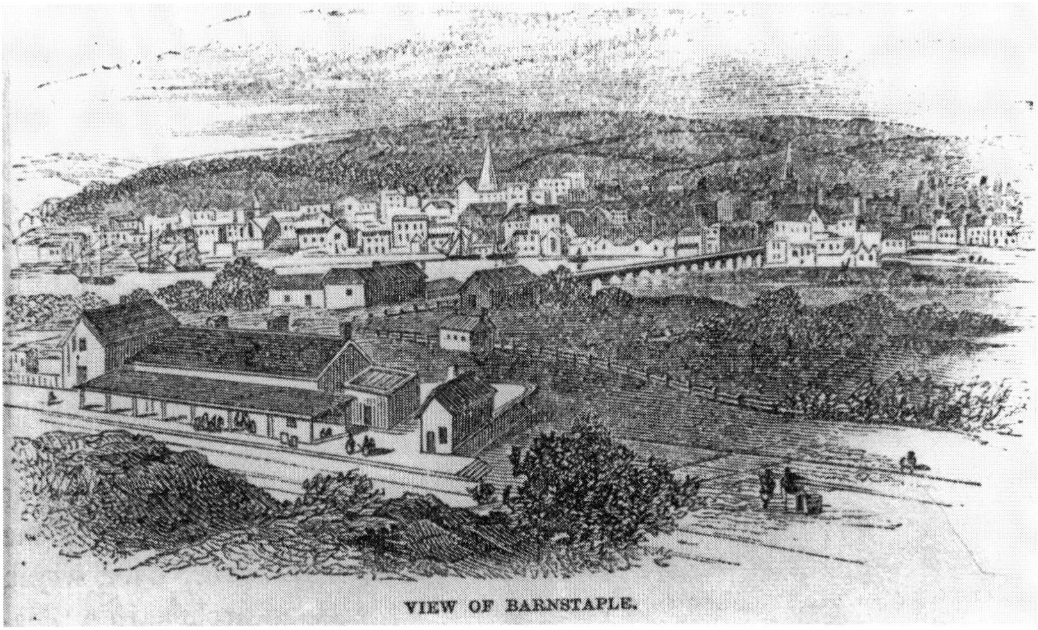

A view of Barnstaple *circa* 1854, the station is in the bottom left hand corner.
Author's collection

promised aid and co-operation (a working agreement had been signed on 11th November, 1869 between the provisional Directors of the Barnstaple & Ilfracombe Railway and the LSWR), but said it would not be willing to find the capital. The Bill was not unopposed, petitions against it being received from Sir William Williams, the Long Bridge Trustees, William Westacott (shipbuilder), some inhabitants of Barnstaple, nineteen persons described as owners, lessees or occupiers of property along the line, and the inhabitants of the district lying to the north of Barnstaple, which derived no benefit from a western line.

An inquiry before the House of Commons Committee was opened on 15th March, 1870.

Archibald Scott, traffic manager of the LSWR, said that more than 30,000 passengers were conveyed to Ilfracombe annually and traffic over the North Devon line had greatly increased: in 1863 it was £15 weekly per mile and in 1869 £22, an increase of 50 per cent. Receipts on the Barnstaple to Bideford line were £13 weekly per mile, and he estimated that the receipts on the Ilfracombe line would be at the very minimum, £12. The 14 miles of line would thus yield £8736 yearly and deducting working expenses, the amount would be £3931 to which would be added the rebate of £2000, making a total of £5931, or more than 5 per cent of £115,000, which was £10,000 more than the estimated expenditure. In addition there would be a considerable volume of goods traffic. William George Beattie, general assistant in the LSWR's loco and carriage department, said that the light railway plan was very suitable for the projected line and was backed by M. McConnel, the Ilfracombe Railway's Consulting Engineer. Galbraith explained the advantages of the Braunton over the Bittadon route and following his exposition, it was announced that Sir William Williams had withdrawn all opposition and had met the promoters "in a liberal spirit". The Bill then passed the committee stage. When this news reached Ilfracombe by telegraph,

> Flags of all nations and colours were suspended across the streets from the houses previously decided upon. Never were so many flags exhibited in the town at one time.
>
> On Saturday evening (19th March) it being understood that the gentlemen who had been to London to give evidence in favour of the railway would return in an omnibus which had been sent to Barnstaple Station to meet them, hundreds of persons stationed themselves in the road leading to Barnstaple, and on the approach of the omnibus, the horses were taken out and some ropes being attached, the vehicle with its occupants

were drawn by the assembled crowd through the town preceded by the band. Amidst tremendous cheering it arrived at the Royal Clarence Hotel, the procession halted and the committee consisting of the Revs W.C. Moore and B. Price, Messrs W.R. Gould and P. Stoneman, briefly addressed the assemblage from the coach roof amidst deafening cheers, after which the crowd dispersed.

The Act was passed on 4th July, 1870 *33-34 Vic. cap 110*, this empowering the railway to run from the LSWR at Barnstaple to Ilfracombe. It could raise a capital of £105,000 and had borrowing powers of £35,000. The line was to be constructed and worked as a light railway within the meaning, and subject to, the provisions of "The Regulation of Railways Act, 1868 ".

Very few local people took shares and the first ordinary meeting of the Barnstaple & Ilfracombe Railway (B&I) was held on 14th October, 1870, when it was reported that "It is a matter of notoriety that the amount of subscriptions forthcoming from the district is so exceedingly small that it would be useless to attempt the construction of the line unless some substantial subsidy can be obtained from the L&SWR." With 40,000 summer visitors invading Ilfracombe, the LSWR Directors were determined that work on the line should begin and sought a method of encouraging subscribers. As far back as 11th November, 1869 they had made an agreement with the B&I which allowed the LSWR to work the line for half the gross receipts and also gave the B&I free use of Barnstaple station. A maximum yearly rebate of £2000 allowed the B&I to pay 5 per cent on debentures and on shares up to £120,000. To speed the sale of B&I shares, in 1871 the LSWR changed the working terms to an inclusive annual rent of £6000 in perpetuity. This move had the anticipated effect of encouraging subscribers who took up all the shares. In 1872 the LSWR Directors cancelled £1275 of their perpetual yearly rental at 23½ years' purchase by accepting the entire issue, which was £30,000, of B&I debenture stock at 4½ per cent (£1275).

James Taylor, who had just completed the Torrington extension, was let the contract for building the line at £90,000. In January 1871 the press reported that

> ... several men are engaged in marking out the intended route of the railway through Braunton.

However, progress was not quite as fast as anticipated. The ceremony of cutting the first sod was carried out at Ilfracombe by Thomas Pain on 27th September, 1871. A procession including the B&I

Directors, LSWR officials, the contractor, Galbraith, bands, banners and a portrait of the late Robert Wreford formed outside the Ilfracombe Hotel and processed in the rain to a field overlooking the town where the station was to be built. On arrival at the grandstand, the vicar blessed the procession and the future works. Pain then placed several spadefuls of earth into a wheelbarrow, pushed it to the end of some planks and tipped it. Several ladies also carried out the same procedure, the special equipment being made from Spanish mahogany by Slocombe, a local cabinetmaker. Additionally, George Hartnoll carried out a similar turf-cutting ceremony at Braunton.

In December the local press reported,

> Something is doing at Braunton in the way of preparation for the Barnstaple to Ilfracombe Railway. Stabling has been provided, a large smiths' shop erected and cottages for the labourers are also being got ready. Many horses and wagons belonging to the contractor have arrived and are daily employed hauling materials towards Ilfracombe, the works having been commenced at two or three points in the parishes of Westdown and Mortehoe. It is expected that a large body of navvies will shortly require to be accommodated in or near this place.

It was also reported that several navvies were at work near the Slade Valley reservoir not far from Ilfracombe.

At the half yearly meeting held 21st February, 1872, Galbraith, the engineer, reported that

> ... the possession of land has been obtained at various points along the course of the railway, and operations commenced by the contractors in the parishes of Pilton, Mortehoe and Ilfracombe. In the first named parish the line is being formed through the property of Mr Rolle by side cutting and in Mortehoe and Ilfracombe wagon roads [i.e. contractor's tramways] have been laid in; and the contractor is opening out the cutting at the summit where about one mile of railway has been formed. The land where possession has been obtained is being fenced off; about a mile of fencing has been erected, and materials for three miles more are on the ground. 130 men and 20 horses are now at work on the railway, and an ample supply of contractor's plant is provided for further operation.

In the building of railways, accidents were a fairly frequent occurrence, and with this particular line, an unusual number were reported in the press. They make interesting reading, revealing much about contemporary construction practices. On 14th February, 1872 a navvy named William King endeavouring to stop one of the tramway wagons in the usual way with a piece of wood thrust through the spokes of a wheel, was involved in an accident when the wood flew out and inflicted a severe wound to his neck. In August Charles Briss, another navvy, was entombed just beyond the Foxhunters Inn when a mass of earth fell on him; both arms were broken and his back severely bruised. Two accidents occurred in April 1873. A navvy was injured while jumping on one of the ballast wagons at Braunton while it was in motion and James Bartlett was working in the deep cutting at Willingcott when a barrow being wheeled along a plank eleven feet above him slipped off, the wheel striking him on the head and knocking him down. The following month James Hutchings was attempting to stop a wagon in Campshot Cutting with a sprag when his left hand became caught between the spokes and forced him to run some distance until the wagon was stopped by his colleagues. In July 1873 came the first recorded fatal injury on the line, this happening when John Crich was killed by a fall of earth. On 13th October there was a further fatal accident at the second cutting from Ilfracombe.

On 12th July, 1874, at about 4.00 pm, 5 men and 2 boys mounted a trolley at the tunnel to ride home at the end of their shift. All went well until they reached the distant signal at Ilfracombe. A long piece of wood was used for propelling and stopping the trolley punt-wise and as they approached the station they tried to stop the trolley, but when the pole was placed in the usual spot it snapped. They tried a second and third time and each time it broke. Two men and both boys jumped off and escaped unhurt, the others not being so lucky. The ballast engine *Gnat* had brought down from the cutting some trucks containing stone and these had been shunted on a siding when the trolley came down at speed. The trolley crashed into them, breaking one of its axles and throwing off the three men. Only two had been actually working on the line, and both were hurt, the others just spectators. The accident occurred through disregard of regulations. The use of the trolley had been forbidden and Sunday work (it happened on a Sunday) was contrary to the orders of the contractor who had given strict instructions that no work was to be done from midnight on Saturday until Monday morning.

Good progress was being made near Ilfracombe. From Cairn Top to Score Tunnel a good bank had been made and attractive ferns and flowers were already springing up on the embankments. Near the reservoir twelve men were at work in a cutting. Progress was continuing on the long summit cutting at Bickington which was the first piece of line to be started and was the last to be completed. In August 1872 twelve of the thirty feet still required excavating and the spoil was being carried towards the reservoir where a heavy embankment was in the course of construction. Galbraith reported that of the twenty-eight cuttings, seven were finished, fifteen were in progress and six had to be commenced. 140,000 cu. yds had been shifted out of a total of 400,000. Thirteen out of the thirty bridges had been built while the construction of the heavy river wall at Barnstaple had commenced and works had advanced rapidly despite the floods. Altogether 4½ miles of railway were formed and partly ballasted, a considerable number of sleepers were on the ground and a cargo of rails daily expected. Near Ilfracombe a short, but very deep cutting had to be made on side-lying ground. The contractor proposed substituting a short tunnel which would expedite the work and involve less risk in future maintenance. Galbraith concurred with this idea and eight or nine men had already driven a heading 200 ft in length, the very hard rock being removed by blasting.

On 20th March the *North Devon Herald* announced that

> ... the new bridge under the Sticklepath Road has been completed and on Tuesday [18th March] operations were renewed at the [Tavistock] end of the iron bridge that is to span the Taw. The long piles that have been daily expected for some weeks arrived on Monday [17th March] and they are now being driven in as fast as circumstances will allow. On the opposite side of the river preparations are made for laying the foundation of the Quay station – in fact, a portion of the concrete bed on which the structure will be raised has already been deposited. The top of the sea wall has been finished to a length of over 250 ft and a further length of over 100 ft is in hand on which the men will work alternately with the station, the latter being reserved for occasions when bad weather or high tides will not permit their remaining on the sea wall. On the Pilton side of the River Yeo the piles for the swing bridge are being sunk and the bank is being completed close up to the spot where the bridge will stand. Further on towards Ilfracombe an accommodation level crossing has been finished between the beach and Capt. Williams's boathouse; while from Braunton onwards the permanent way is being laid as rapidly as possible.

In October the Barnstaple paper said that

> More than half of the iron bridge is so far completed as to enable temporary rails to be laid along it; the diversion of the long bridge is rapidly progressing; the new portion of road which is to supersede that now used at the Tawstock end of the bridge is being metalled and made ready for use; the station building on the quay, so far as passenger traffic is concerned, will in a few weeks be ready for occupation; the new iron bridge across the Pilton cut has been commenced; and generally, extensive progress has been made since our last report.

On 24th January, 1874 The *Ilfracombe Chronicle* reported that the tunnel was finished for half its length, final completion being anticipated in

March. This estimate proved to be accurate, as a small four-coupled tank engine named *Gnat* and ten wagons passed through the tunnel for the first time on 16th March. *Gnat* must have been brought by road, as the summit cutting was yet to be completed and many men were at work there, slowly excavating through the rock. From Mortehoe to Barnstaple the railway was finished, and on 15th January a locomotive and wagons ran from Pottington Point, Barnstaple to Mortehoe, which was the longest journey so far performed.

In March 1874 the D&S announced its intention of opening an office at Ilfracombe and running a connecting service to Barnstaple for passengers and goods additional to that run by other promoters. The service began on 1st June with three trips daily in each direction taking 1½ hours, the four-horse brakes (large passenger wagonettes) being supplied by Perry of Stokes Croft, Bristol. The D&S was forced to take this competitive step as the LSWR would not allow through bookings to its line from LSWR stations. Additionally, when the Ilfracombe line was opened, a connecting bus service was operated between the D&S and LSWR stations at Barnstaple, and using the D&S route the fastest time between London and Ilfracombe was 7 hrs 30 mins. The LSWR had had a combined booking clerk/manager in an office at Ilfracombe since 1869.

Contractor's engine at Ilfracombe 1874; from an invitation ticket to the opening dinner.
Ilfracombe Museum

At Barnstaple a huge mass of rock had been moved from the south side of Barnstaple Junction station, and a new 400 ft long platform erected for down trains in its place. Hitherto there had only been a single platform. About 7.00 pm on 16th June, 1874, hundreds of Barumites (residents of Barnstaple, the town being locally known as "Barum") watched the first locomotive cross the iron bridge. The following day The *Bristol Times & Mirror* recorded that "Last night an engine laden with ballast and also carrying a freight of navvies and railway officials, made a testing trip over the iron bridge (of surpassing ugliness), which spans the river Taw." Two days later a "large heavy goods engine" weighing about 30 tons including the tender [probably an "Ilfracombe Goods" engine which actually weighed 35 tons 17½ cwt] was driven across and back again. On the Tawstock side it took aboard W. Jacomb, the LSWR Engineer, Fisher, the District Engineer, and Mair, the contractor's agent, and all were taken to Mortehoe.

On 2nd July The *North Devon Herald* reported that the summit cutting near Ilfracombe was completed on Saturday last (27th June).

> On Sunday afternoon, the men all being at work, the ballast engine *Whitmore* which was also at work, came from Barnstaple direct through the (summit) cutting to our station with trucks, etc., these being the first engine and trucks

Opening of the railway in 1874 – triumphal arch in Station Drive, Ilfracombe.
Ilfracombe Museum

that have come through. On arriving at the block signal box, which has been slated and the windows glazed, I noticed twelve levers fixed inside for the signals and points which will be worked by a signalman inside the box. The turn-table has been put in and the engine shed is being roofed.

The first "passenger" train over the line arrived at Ilfracombe at 6.20 pm on 30th June, drawn by two beflagged "Ilfracombe Goods" engines, No. 283 piloting No. 282. The train consisted of one first, one third and four second class coaches with two brake vans, the latter having "Barnstaple and Ilfracombe" prominently painted on them in addition to the initials of the LSWR. The coaches were ballasted with iron chairs, the total weight of the train amounting to some 130 tons. It stopped at all stations and railway officials and James Taylor, the contractor, inspected the swing bridge over the Yeo and at stations, signal boxes and other features. At Braunton station one of the engines was detached, the train being taken on by a single engine. On reaching the incline between Foxhunters Inn and Mortehoe station, the train engine was detached and the coaches allowed to run down the incline of 1 in 40 by themselves. The brakes were then applied and the coaches halted. This test was tried on other gradients. The whole trip, including stoppages, took about 2½ hours. Hundreds of people greeted its arrival at Ilfracombe. The return journey took about an hour. It was found that one engine could easily haul the load of 83 tons up the bank of 1 in 36.

The Board of Trade inspection of the 14 miles 65.8 chains line was carried out on 13th July by Col. C.S. Hutchinson. He was conveyed from St David's, Exeter, to Barnstaple by special train and began his inspection about 8.00 am accompanied by Messrs Scott, Galbraith, Jacomb, Church, Fisher, Tyler and Higgs of the LSWR and Taylor the contractor. Testing the long iron bridge at Barnstaple took about two hours. Two locomotives weighing a total of 80 tons formed the load which passed backwards and forwards across the bridge, the inspector measuring the deflection with his theodolite. The inspection train consisted of a locomotive, two coaches, brake van and another engine at the rear. It was nearly 3.00 pm before the train arrived at Ilfracombe where it was welcomed by a large crowd. The inspecting party was met by a drag (a four-horse private vehicle, like a stage coach) and three horses from the Clarence Hotel and taken to the Ilfracombe Hotel for a late lunch, after which Ilfracombe station was inspected. Barnstaple was reached at 6.00 pm.

In his report passing the line, Col. Hutchinson said that the line was single throughout, no provision being made for doubling. The wrought iron viaduct over the Taw had 17 spans varying in width from 30 to 110 ft and constructed on a curve of 7½ chains radius which was the sharpest on the branch. The girders were supported on Hughes's wrought iron piles braced together with timber. The main girders were plate, 4 ft in depth and made the viaduct strong enough for ordinary engines to use. The swing bridge across the Yeo was 110 ft long and to avoid unnecessary weight had been constructed for light engines and under passage of these gave moderate deflections. He found the bridge slow to open. There were 21 underline bridges, 17 of which had timber tops resting on masonry abutments (when the line was doubled these were replaced with a bridge built entirely of stone or brick), others with a larger span being built of masonry. There were eight level crossings. In consequence of the steep gradients on which Ilfracombe is approached, the LSWR provided special brake vans which were run in addition to the ordinary vans with every train between Braunton and Ilfracombe.

A time sheet of the GWR horse-bus from Barnstaple to Ilfracombe on 16th June, 1884. This was prior to the opening of the loop line at Barnstaple which allowed the running of through trains. Note the time taken by the bus considerably exceeds that mentioned on *Page 27*.

Author's collection

Chapter Two

The Line Opens

A public meeting was held on 7th July to discuss celebrating the opening of the railway. It was a considerate thought that celebrations should not take place on the opening day as this would be an anxious one for the railway company. The first public train to use the line was the 6.35 am on 20th July, 1874 from Ilfracombe, headed by No. 282 hauling 12 coaches and banked in the rear by No. 283. On the opening day several Barumites, to avoid the anticipated rush at the Quay station, walked to the Junction there to wait for the first train, the 7.00 am from Exeter, and as it drew up, heard for the first time the shout, "Change here for Ilfracombe". The 9.10 am from Barnstaple consisted of 13 coaches drawn by two locomotives. Passing over the long iron bridge detonators exploded making "nervous parties fear the structure was snapping under them". Reaching the 1 in 40 incline to Mortehoe "the two little locomotives ascended it as if there was no burden at all at their backs." At Mortehoe station a small boy, frightened of going on board the train, was thrust into a third class compartment by one of the guards. The train was welcomed to Ilfracombe by the bells of the parish church.

Ilfracombe station was decorated with flags and mottoes used previously at Windsor for the reception of the Czar and Czarina of Russia. Banners read: "Welcome VR" and "Welcome AM" (Alexander II and Maria). The platform and roof pillars were turned into Venetian masts, being striped with coloured cloth and the platform roof festooned with artificial flowers. A triumphal arch on the station approach road read: "United in Bonds of Iron". Two omnibuses met the trains: a four-horse bus from the Ilfracombe Hotel and a bus from the Clarence Hotel. A tea was held in the Market for "aged people and schoolchildren of the town". A public dinner to celebrate the opening was held at the Ilfracombe Hotel on 21st July. The mayors of Barnstaple, Bideford, Torrington and South Molton, together with LSWR officials, were greeted at the station and processed to the banquet. A public promenade, ball, illuminations and rural sports were organised for the evening and beacon fires lighted on the hills. At 1.30 pm on the following day a "cold collation" was provided for about 150 navvies who had worked on the line at the Ilfracombe end, while those on the Barnstaple-Braunton section were entertained to supper at the Golden Fleece, Barnstaple, on 25th July. Messrs Attwood & Co., outfitters of Ilfracombe, celebrated the opening by having a medal struck.

The opening of the line certainly helped the district's economy. On 27th July an Ilfracombe butcher went by rail to a sale near Exeter and bought prime wether sheep and lambs, fat bullocks and calves. The following day they arrived at Ilfracombe still in prime condition. This would have been impossible before the opening of the railway except at the cost of three times the time and probably ten times the money for road expenses.

Some people did not adapt themselves to the railway quite so quickly. One yokel saw a train near the tunnel at Ilfracombe. He described vividly how he "zeed un comin' up along, with vour or vive, or vive or six carriages behind mun; her puffed and blowed and come on an' on till her got nearly close up to where I waz standin' and then all at once when un zeed me, her was vrightened and bolted into a hole i' th' wall" (*Ilfracombe Chronicle*, 1st August, 1874).

On 13th August Mortehoe station was seriously damaged by fire; the booking office, waiting room, telegraph office and porters' room were destroyed including instruments, papers and tickets, only the swift action of stationmaster Rice and his family saved their home. While the station was being rebuilt, office work was carried out in a "rickety temporary erection".

On 11th September the summit cutting gave trouble when the last train of the day, the 8.35 pm from Barnstaple, ran into a landslip consisting of about two tons of earth, but luckily no damage was done or any one injured. As a safety measure a watchman was stationed in the cutting. On 19th March, 1875 the watchman discovered that his hut was on fire and with the last down train due, he took his lamp and proceeded towards Mortehoe and managed to stop the train which then proceeded cautiously towards Ilfracombe, but it was found that the line was clear and none of the timbers of the hut, which was situated close to the track, would foul the train.

Meanwhile, in accordance with an agreement of 1st April, 1874, the LSWR by an Act of *37-38 Vic. cap 143*, dated 16th July, 1874, acquired the B&I by the issue of £30,000 LSWR 4½ per cent perpetual debenture stock and £105,000 LSWR 4½ per cent "Ilfracombe Rentcharge Stock" equalling the £6,000 the B&I received under the 1871-72 agreements. The actual amalgamation took place in 1875.

The Ilfracombe Branch ceased to be a light railway in 1887, though because of the severe gradients the overall speed restriction remained 25 mph. The LSWR found that traffic on the line was sufficiently heavy to warrant doubling, and a contract for this to be carried out was let to Messrs Lucas & Aird, though the section from Pottington to

Barnstaple Junction had to be left single because of the prohibitive expense of doubling the swing bridge and the long iron bridge. Lucas & Aird's contract was for £40,000 and work began in August 1888. Although land had been acquired for double track, when the line was originally built it was rather short-sightedly built in the centre of this, so that doubling necessitated the acquisition of more land in several places. The overbridges had to be demolished and rebuilt and the gatekeeper's cottage at Stoney Bridge level crossing was razed to the ground to make way for the second line and a large lodge built nearby. All stone for bridges and ballasting was taken from a quarry near Foxhunters Inn. Platforms at Braunton and Mortehoe were raised about a foot and lengthened.

The first section to be completed was from Braunton to Mortehoe on 1st July, 1889. This had necessitated the reconstruction of four overbridges and the widening of nine underbridges. On 7th June, 1890 blasting operations west of the tunnel caused 20 tons of rock to fall across the track. The 10.10 am train, heavily laden with LSWR and GWR coaches, had already left Ilfracombe. It was stopped and reversed back to the terminus and held there for over an hour until

Barnstaple Quay station *circa* 20th July, 1874, it was renamed Barrnstaple Town in July 1886.
Author's collection

the line was cleared. The double line from Braunton to Pottington was opened on 4th August, 1890. This section was spanned by two overbridges and crossed five underbridges which required widening. A second platform was provided at Wrafton station and a signal box opened at Pottington. Work on doubling the Mortehoe-Ilfracombe section was very heavy as the cuttings were deep and the soil rocky, but the second track was opened on 1st July, 1891.

Meanwhile the Great Blizzard of 1891 had caused trouble. On 9th March the train due in at Ilfracombe at 9.08 pm was trapped in a 12 ft deep drift by the bridge 200 yds north of Mortehoe station, its passengers sheltering in the nearby Fortescue Hotel and the station master's house. A telegram was despatched to Mr Heather, the superintendent at Barnstaple and about 11.00 pm a relief train containing twenty men set off. This became embedded in a huge drift near the Foxhunters Inn, snow drifting in cuttings to a depth of nearly twenty feet and completely covering the relief train. The gang, unable to return to Braunton, made its way to Mortehoe station. By this time the Fortescue Hotel was running short of provisions so the relief gang proceeded to walk 2¾ miles to West Down to procure food.

Ilfracombe station from The Cairn c. 1895. Much of the lengthened platform lacks a canopy. The goods shed is in the foreground, the engine shed on the right of the station complex.

Ilfracombe Museum

THE LINE OPENS

Between 60 and 100 men, including some of Lucas & Aird's employees and working under Permanent Way Inspector Palmer of Barnstaple, cleared the up line to Mortehoe which enabled the 3.29 pm to run from Barnstaple as far as Mortehoe. The forty men working on doubling the line, using their light engines and an improvised snow plough, released the Monday train on Wednesday night, and also enabled the 6.00 pm from Barnstaple to run through to Ilfracombe. The Barnstaple to Braunton section was unaffected by snow and a normal service was run on this stretch of line. (The severe winter of 1947 saw another train being snowed up under the overbridge near Mortehoe, while a blizzard at the end of 1962 closed the line for a day.)

'Ilfracombe Goods' No. 283 leaving Ilfracombe *c.* 1907. A GWR coach in the siding emphasises the gradient of 1 in 36. The notice on the right reads "Speed 4 mph".

F.E. Box

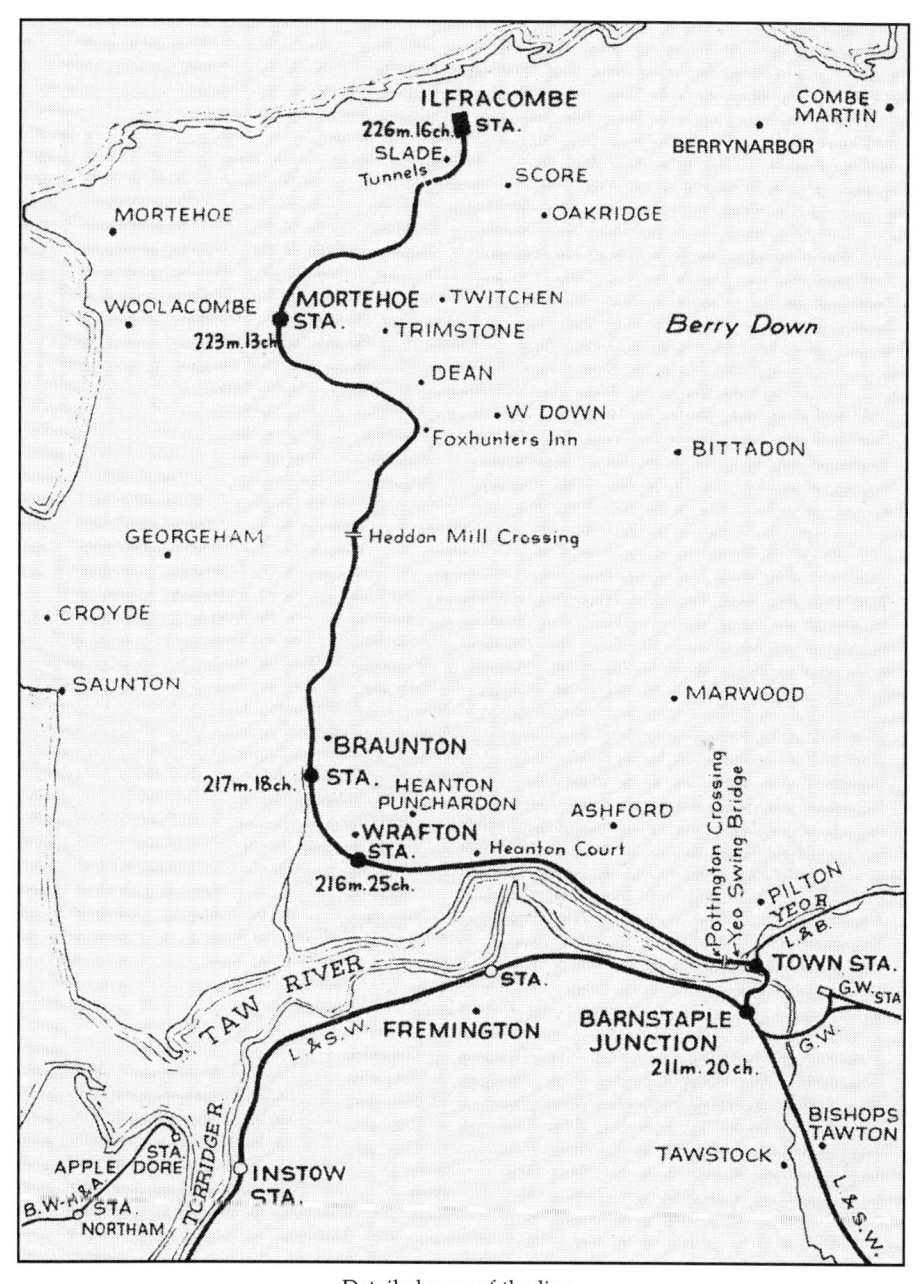

Detailed map of the line.

Chapter Three

Description of the Line

The Ilfracombe line, 14 miles 74 chains in length, started from Barnstaple Junction. The stone-built station designed by Sir William Tite, chairman of the Exeter & Crediton Railway and architect of London's Royal Exchange, was built by the North Devon Railway. Scattered openings in large expanses of wall gave the station a rather gaunt appearance. It had three platforms, the main office building being adjacent to platform No. 1 which had a refreshment room. The island platform (Nos. 2 and 3), and 400 feet in length, was opened in May 1874 in readiness for the Ilfracombe line. In a rationalisation scheme which came into operation on 26th April, 1971, platform 1 was made a terminal and on 21st May, 1971 platform 3 was taken out of use. Gas lighting and a footbridge to the island platform survived until the late nineteen seventies, this platform being denuded of its buildings c.1980. A travel centre opened in 1981, while the following year the station was sensitively restored, great care being taken to blend new material with the original and not disturb its overall appearance, moulds being taken from the original window surrounds so that exact replicas could be made. At the up end

The deserted Barnstaple Junction at 11.20 am on 25th June, 1925. Not a passenger in sight. The Ilfracombe Branch curves sharply right, the Bideford line left. Barnstaple Junction West Signal Box stands at the bifurcation. The solid mode of construction for the up platform canopy can clearly be seen. Notice the step to assist porters crossing the track between platforms. The 'C' on the bracket signal is the speed restriction commencement board for the Ilfracombe route. *British Railways*

Barnstaple West signal box stands at the junction of the lines to Ilfracombe (*right*) and Bideford (*left*) in October 1907. The box was unusually tall in order to allow the signalman a view over the road bridge. The sign at the foot of the signal box steps reads: "Maximum speed 15 miles per hour to Town Station". *F.E. Box*

A more modern view taken in June 1925 of the photograph above. The tall signal box has been replaced by one of normal height and set at a slightly different angle. Note the check rails on the sharp curves; the mass of point rodding, and trap point on the left hand siding. On the right a wagon turntable gives access to a number of short sidings, vehicles being shunted by horse. Just beyond the right hand overbridge the line becomes single to Pottington. Through the left hand bridge wagons stand on the saw mill siding. On the far left the carriage way leads down to the platform. *British Railways*

of the station the spur to the GWR station diverged south of the "A" signal box, while at the down end was the junction of the Torrington and Ilfracombe branches near "B" box. Prior to 2nd October, 1949 these cabins were called "East" and "West" respectively. Barnstaple West signal box was a tall structure to enable the signalman to see over the adjacent road bridge. It was later replaced by a lower box. The station possessed quite an extensive goods yard, one of the sidings serving a manure store, later a slaughter house. Private sidings served the Blue Circle Cement depot.

Barnstaple Junction was the main locomotive depot for the area, and the timber-built shed equipped with a small workshop, and (in later days) a coal stage. The original turntable was replaced c.1890 by one of 50 ft diameter. As this was not long enough to hold an engine of the West Country class, it was necessary to run such a locomotive to Ilfracombe to be turned there. Barnstaple Junction had the code 72E in BR (Southern Region) days, Torrington and Ilfracombe being sub sheds. When the area was transferred to the Western Region on 1st January, 1963, the code was changed to 83F. On 31st December, 1922, the eve of amalgamation, 13 engines were shedded at Barnstaple. In 1926 the shed employed a staff of 45, including 13 pairs of drivers and firemen. The depot closed in August 1964.

Barnstaple Junction, view down *circa* 1914. The engine shed is on the right and the goods shed in the centre. *Author's collection*

Reproduced courtesy of The Ordnance Survey map of 1904.

Adams '460' class 4-4-0 at Barnstaple Junction on a wet 25th July, 1925. Notice the storm sheet between the cab and the tender. Placed on the duplicate list om May 1912, No. 0462 was withdrawn in April 1926. Barnstaple East signal box is in the background.

H.C. Casserley

'West Country' class Pacific No. 34002 *Salisbury* rounds the curve before reaching the viaduct, 1st August, 1952. *R.E. Toop*

A Barnstaple Junction to
Barnstaple Town single line
tablet.
Author's collection

Between the station and the "B" signal box the line bifurcated, the Ilfracombe line diverging to the north west, almost immediately passing under a bridge carrying the A39 road, the line becoming single track with electric token working and beyond was the facing siding to Raleigh Cabinet Works. The siding, opened May 1890 and worked by a two-lever ground frame unlocked by the train staff, was taken out of use on 8th December, 1966. The gates of the level crossing to the works and those of a footpath which led to Anchor Woods were both controlled by a gateman stationed at the latter crossing.

The River Taw was spanned by a wrought iron bridge 213 yds in length curving through ninety degrees. It consisted of 15 pairs of main girders each 40 ft in length with a weight of 6 tons resting on wrought iron piers sunk to a considerable depth in the sands of the river bed and filled in below with concrete. At the north end of the bridge was the Quay station, 46 chains from Barnstaple Junction and saving the town residents a lengthy walk across the Long Bridge and in July 1886 it was renamed Barnstaple Town. The station was in a cramped position and had no sidings being closed on 16th May, 1898 on the opening of the new Barnstaple Town station 11 chains to the north. The new station was required as the original was unsuited for adaptation for use by the 1 ft 11½ in. gauge Lynton & Barnstaple Railway, opened on 16th May, 1898 (*see Oakwood Library No. 51*). Barnstaple Corporation provided land for the new station in exchange for the site of the old one. The standard gauge platform, 500 ft in length, was situated on the east side of the main line, the east face for the majority of its length being used as a

DESCRIPTION OF THE LINE 43

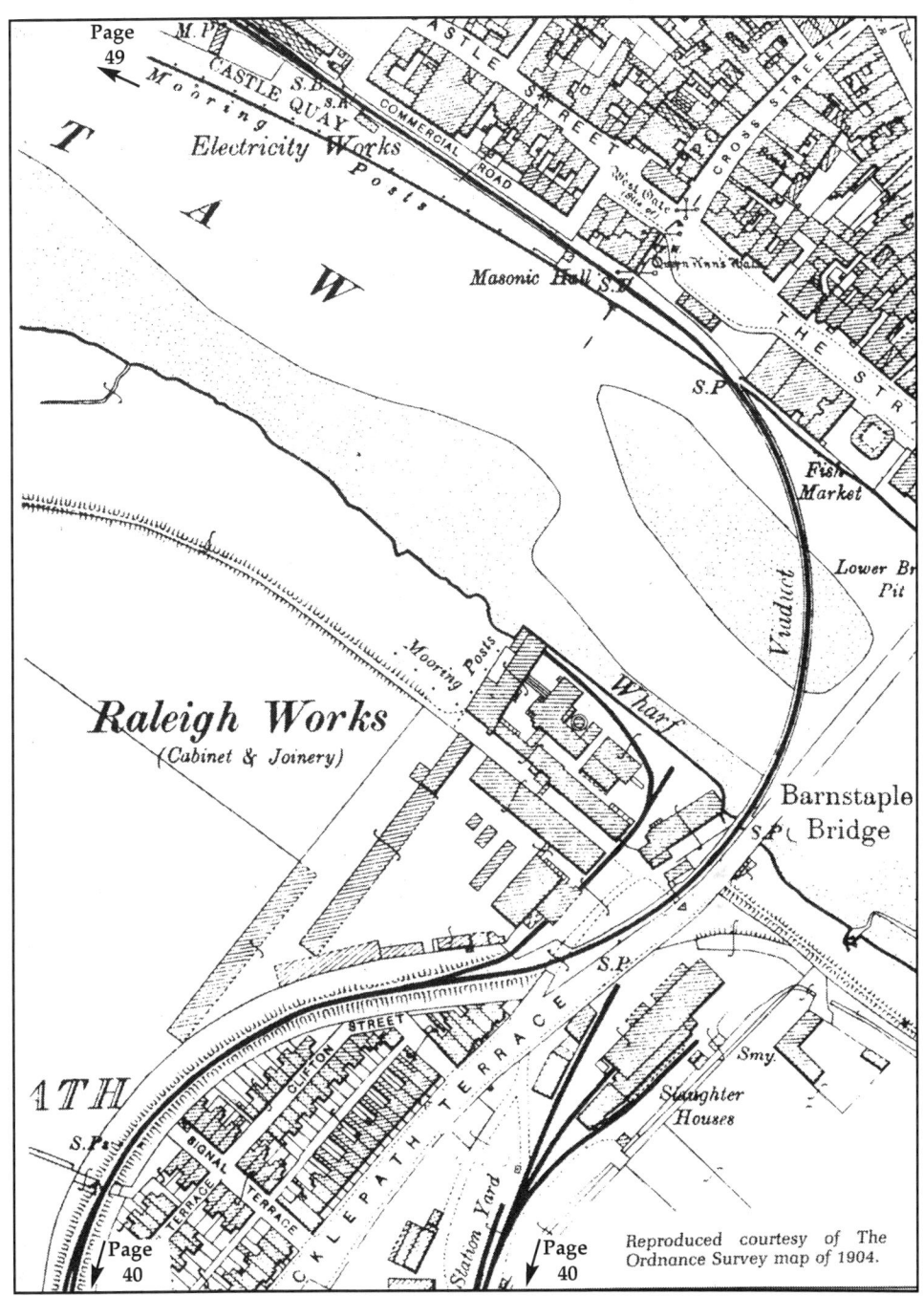

Reproduced courtesy of The Ordnance Survey map of 1904.

A post-closure view of the Taw viaduct looking towards Barnstaple Town station. Notice how the girder tops on the right allowed railwaymen to take refuge from an approaching train. Note also the check railed curve and the telegraph wires supported along the outside of the girder sides. *R.W. Kidner*

'M7' class 0-4-4T No. 250 heads an up train with a GWR through coach from Ilfracombe to Paddington closest to the engine, 15th July, 1935. *S.W. Baker*

DESCRIPTION OF THE LINE 45

An Adams 0-4-4T crosses the bridge in October 1907 with a train of LSWR and GWR four and six-wheel coaches. The building of the closed Barnstaple Quay station is to the left of the locomotive. *F.E. Box*

Barnstaple Quay station, view up, pre -1898. To the right an 0-6-0 hauls a passenger train across the bridge. *Author's collection*

Ex-GWR '43XX' class 2-6-0, No. 5336 pauses at Barnstaple Town with the 09.25 Ilfracombe to Taunton local passenger service on the 15th August, 1964. Lack of a smokebox door number and shed plates recalls the scene of some 20 years before, marred only by the presence of the flat-bottomed rails visible. *E. Wilmshurst*

2-6-2T No. 188 *Lew* at Barnstaple Town, heads a mixed narrow gauge train, on the Lynton and Barnstaple Railway, *circa* 1935. *Author's collection*

The standard and narrow gauge transhipment sidings at Barnstaple Town.
C. Graseman

terminus by L&B trains, and it was for this reason that the station building had to be sited at the extreme southern end of the station. The station buildings had a frontage of 114 ft and were constructed of dressed stone from Chestwood Quarries, Newport, Barnstaple; the facings and chimneys being of Bath stone. The steel framed and glazed platform canopy carried on cast iron columns extended 150 ft northwards from the building to shelter both the Lynton & Barnstaple Railway and LSWR passengers; but after closure of the narrow gauge line, this canopy was shortened almost to the station building and an SR style valance end fitted. The goods transfer dock was merely a timber platform situated between narrow gauge and standard gauge rails. Following closure of the L&B on 30th September, 1935, this exchange siding was lifted on 3rd April, 1940, though the points were retained, a spur leading to a sand drag to protect trains from the open swing bridge. The passing loop, removed in January 1964, was useless for passenger trains as it had no platform, there being insufficient space between it and the quay to provide one. An economy could have been made in 1935 by closing Barnstaple Town signal box, for with the abandonment of the narrow gauge line, the function of the standard gauge signal box really ceased, its chief purpose being to provide access to the exchange siding. Today the station building is a restaurant; flats for retired folk have been built on the down end of the platform, while the signal box is now the Lynton & Barnstaple Railway Association Museum. The site of the narrow gauge terminus is marked by a plaque.

The single line crossed the River Yeo over a swing bridge which allowed shipping access to Rolle Quay and Pilton Wharf (L&BR). Pottington Swing Bridge, locally known as Pill Bridge, was 59 ft in length and 14 ft wide, and the channel capable of being negotiated by any ship up to 250 tons burden. To open the bridge the fishplates holding the rails in position were required to be disconnected, and three platelayers by means of a rack and pinion gear, slewed the bridge round. It resembled a turntable, revolving on a centre cogged spindle through 180 degrees. As the bridge did not turn on its centre, one end was counter-balanced, the weight of the bridge being carried by three small wheels running on a race.

The signalman was required to be present when the bridge was opened. To ensure safety, no up train was allowed to leave Braunton station during the time the bridge was open to the waterway and down trains were only allowed to proceed as far as Barnstaple Town. When the bridge was closed to trains it was locked by two mechanical locking bolts, one at each end, controlled by Sykes's electrical locking gear from Pottington signal box. On 19th August, 1891 a vessel grounded against the bridge and could not be refloated until the next tide. This blocked the railway and difficulty was experienced in dealing with the heavy summer traffic. Fortunately one engine remained on the Ilfracombe side

Pottington Swing Bridge in open position: view towards Wrafton, 10th June, 1977.

Author

DESCRIPTION OF THE LINE

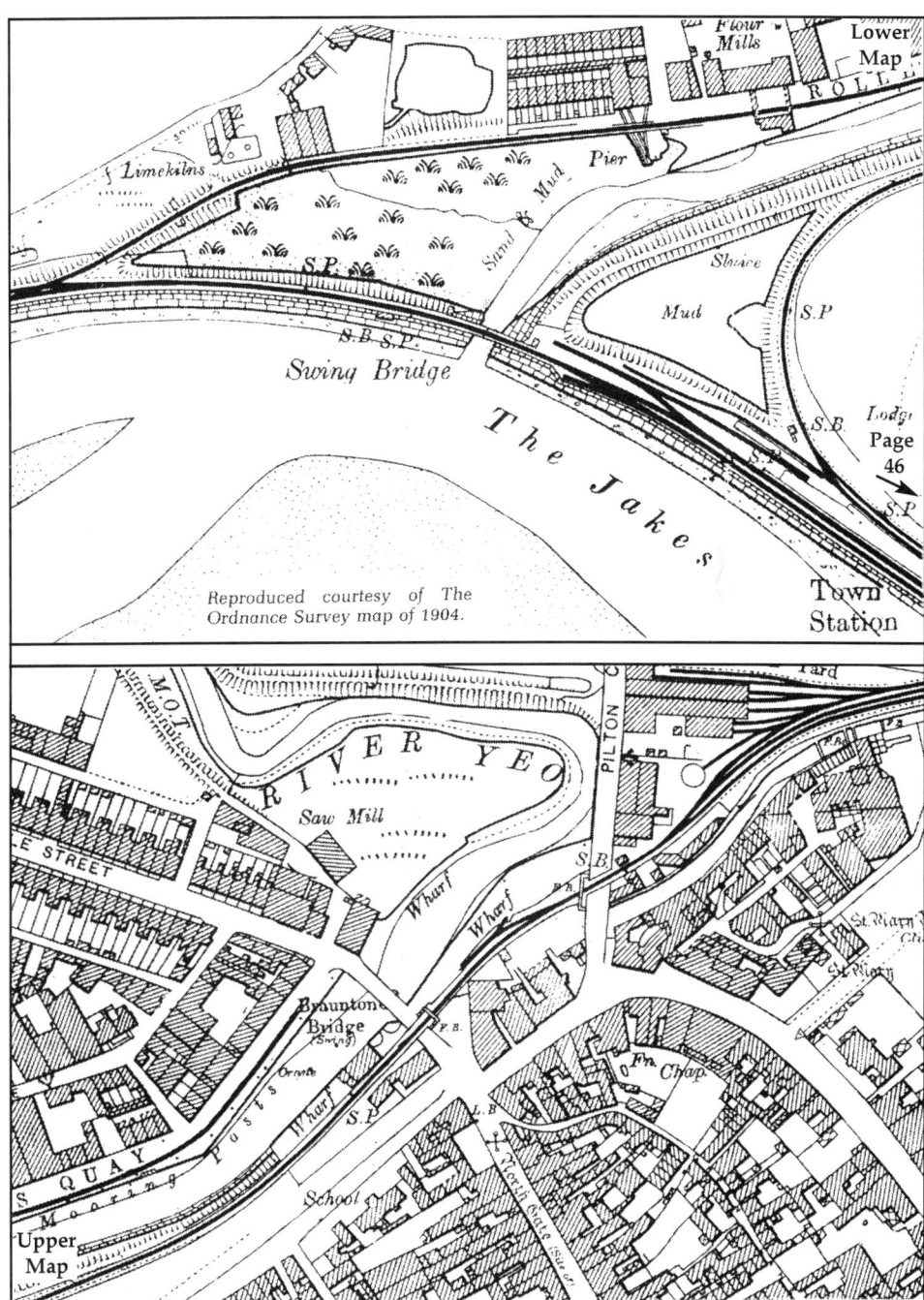

Reproduced courtesy of The Ordnance Survey map of 1904.

of the bridge and could therefore work trains to and from the northern side of the bridge at Pottington where passengers were transferred by road to the trains on the other side.

At Pottington signal box the line became double. The box was reduced to a ground frame on 17th December, 1967. Beyond the cabin a trailing junction led to the Rolle Quay siding, 26 chains in length. Traffic at this quay was principally grain and flour. The siding was closed on 7th September, 1964 and taken out of use on 24th January, 1965. With the singling of the track on 17th December, 1967 the former up line was used between Pottington and Braunton. The track ran along the north bank of the River Taw for the first two miles being carried on an embankment built on marshy ground. After passing Strand House, at Ashford it crossed a small bridge that allowed vehicles access to the river bank. Beyond Heanton Court the railway turned inland passing the housing estate serving RAF Chivenor which could have warranted a halt for residents needing to travel to Braunton or Barnstaple for shopping or business. The line ran alongside the airfield, but the opportunity of laying a siding for fuel tank wagons was lost, all of it arriving by road.

Wrafton (5 miles 2 ch.) originally had a siding but no passing loop. On doubling, it became a simple two-road station with two goods sidings at the up end of the down platform. One of the sidings was used during the summer for two six-berth camping coaches; in 1955 the rental varied from £5 15s. 0d. per week during the low season to £9 in the height of the summer. The other siding was sometimes used by the RAF. Both sidings were taken out of use on 15th February, 1965. The station master's house (now a private dwelling) and station offices were on the up platform. The station walls, like those of Braunton and Mortehoe, were rendered with cement during the period of Southern Railway ownership. On the down platform stood a shelter and signal box. Wrafton down distant was the only colour-light signal on the branch. The box was reduced to a ground frame on 17th December, 1967 and damaged by fire a few months after the line closed. The hand-wheel which swung the level crossing gates was transferred to Tisbury on the Salisbury-Exeter line.

Braunton for Saunton Sands and Croyde Bay (5 miles 75 ch.) until doubling, was a passing place on the single line. The main buildings were situated on the down platform, which was short compared with the up. On the up side was the goods shed, cattle dock and five sidings, while at the east end of the down side were two sidings used by waiting banking engines. These were principally required only on summer Saturdays, when as many as three could be seen waiting there, as the

DESCRIPTION OF THE LINE

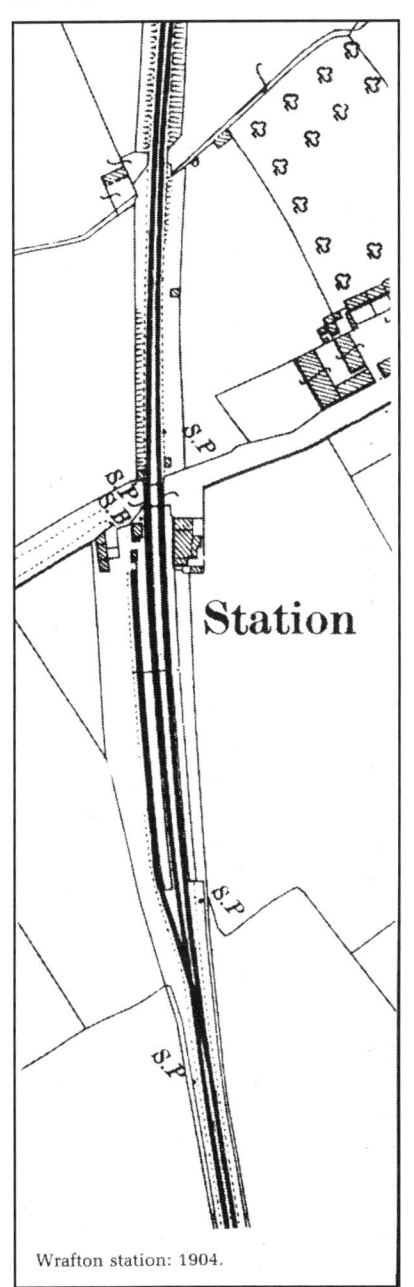

Wrafton station: 1904.

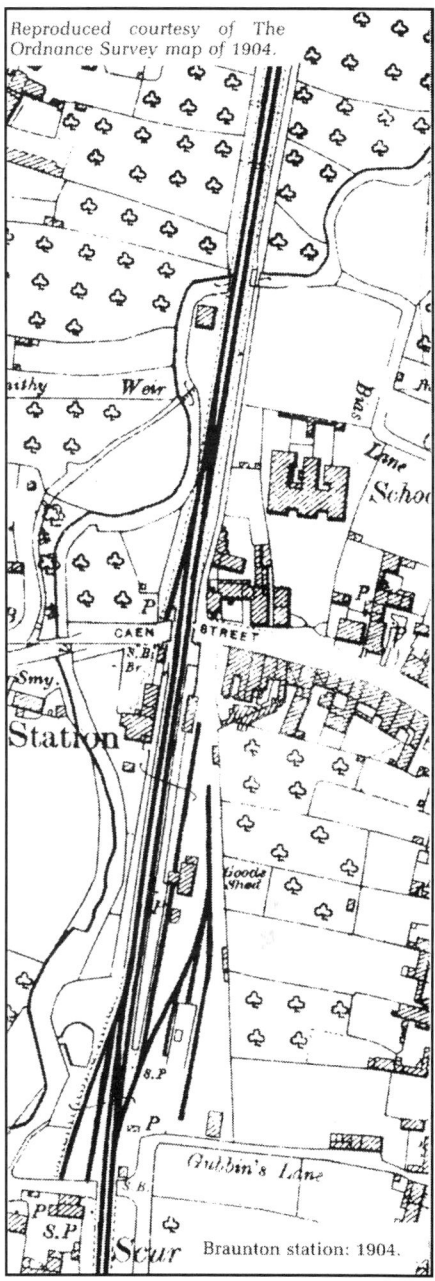

Reproduced courtesy of The Ordnance Survey map of 1904.

Braunton station: 1904.

52   THE BARNSTAPLE AND ILFRACOMBE RAILWAY

The up platform of Wrafton station.   *Lens of Sutton*

The down platform of Wrafton station looking towards Barnstaple; signal box and waiting shelter right, with goods siding beyond.   *Lens of Sutton*

gradient of 1 in 74 began just beyond the station. A train requiring a banker drew forward over the level crossing to await its attachment. Water cranes situated on both platforms were fed from a large water tower, the supply being pumped from the River Caen. The siding at the west end of the down platform was used for oil tank wagons. All the sidings were taken out of use by 6th April, 1965. In 1967 Seymour Cobley despatched 15,000 to 20,000 packages of blooms from the station to distant urban markets, this traffic requiring three or four vans daily in the height of the season. The former station house is now a newsagent's.

When the line was singled, north of the station the road used changed from the former up, to the former down line. Although the line passed within 200 yds of the centre of Knowle, the village was never provided with a halt. The line reached Stoney Bridge Crossing, not a block post, and beyond was Heddon Mill Crossing signal box opened as a block post c.1889 to break up the long section of 5 miles 70 ch. between Braunton and Mortehoe. A crossover was sited here until 1920. The box was reduced to a ground frame on 17th December, 1967. The gradient steepened to 1 in 40 and this continued, with brief respites, for 3¼ miles to Mortehoe, 600 feet above sea level.

View of Braunton looking towards Ilfracombe c. 1935.   *Author's collection*

Two views of Braunton (for Saunton Sands and Croyde Bay) looking towards Ilfracombe. Note the water column at the end of the platform. *Lens of Sutton*

Mortehoe (11 miles 65 ch.), originally spelt Morthoe, became Mortehoe on 13th May, 1902 and was re-named Mortehoe and Woolacombe on 5th June, 1950. Originally a passing place on the single line, it had two upside sidings and five on the down side, all being lifted by 1966. The station master's house, booking office and signal box were on the down platform, the up platform being provided with a shelter. The down platform had a dull cement-rendered building to which a plain canopy had been added. The station was especially active on summer Saturdays when it was possible for trains entering it from both directions to be banked, so that in addition to despatching the trains, the bankers were required to be returned. All tickets were collected at Mortehoe until about 1925 when Ilfracombe was made a closed station. The station building now restored, is part of a leisure centre, two wheel-less coaches stand at each platform and, particularly in the half light, one can imagine that trains still run.

When the line was singled, north of the station the road changed from the former down to the up line. A feature of the B&I is a low retaining wall at the foot of the embankments of certain cuttings, these walls, like the overbridges, being built of stone. An example of this walling can be seen beyond the station in Summit Cutting, the cause of so much trouble in early days and marking the beginning of the 2¼ mile long bank of

An early view of the down platform of Morethoe (for Woolacome and Lee) looking towards Ilfracombe, in 1907. Note the 'barley sugar' lamp post. The down platform canopy has yet to be erected. *F.E. Box*

BR Standard class '4' 2-6-4T No. 80039 arriving at Mortehoe with the Ilfracombe section of the Southern Counties Society's "Exeter Flyer" on 12th September, 1965. Notice how the tracks fall out of sight on a gradient of 1 in 40, rather than disappear into the distance.

R.E. Toop

'43XX' class 2-6-0 No. 6346, leaves Mortehoe with the 08.50 Taunton to Ilfracombe train on 27th July, 1963. At the rear of the train the canopy erected on the down platform can be seen.

P.W. Gray

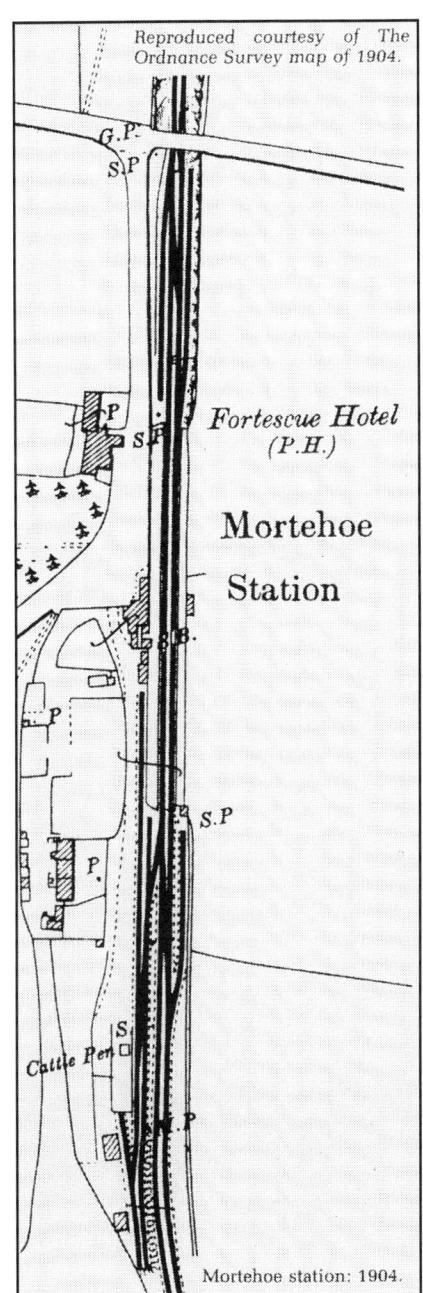

Mortehoe station: 1904.

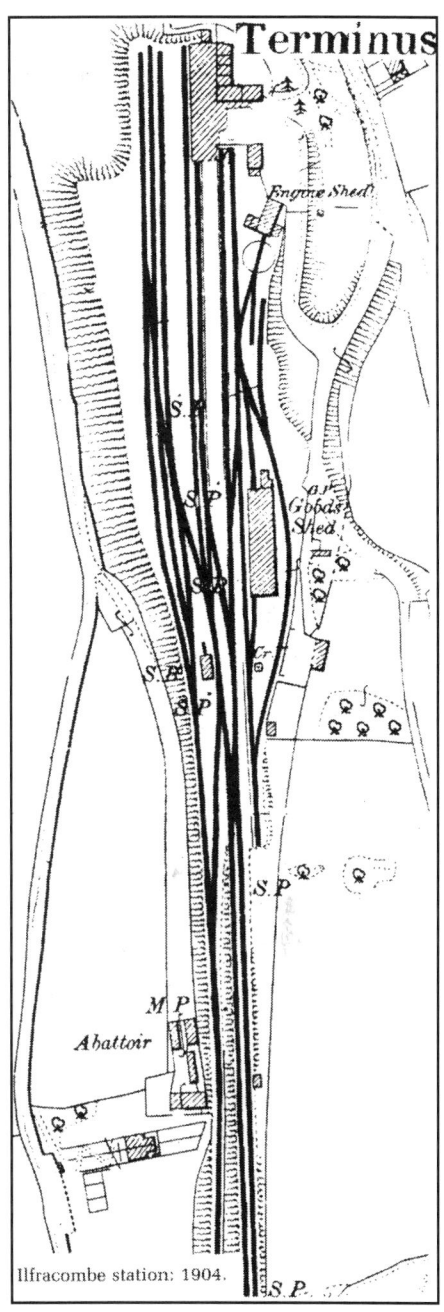

Ilfracombe station: 1904.

'N' class 2-6-0, No. 31818 banking the up "Atlantic Coast Express" past the Slade Reservoir on 1st September, 1962. The train's locomotive was 'Battle of Britain' class Pacific No. 34072 *Squadron*. *P.W. Gray*

'M7' class 0-4-4T No. 30667 and '43XX' class 2-6-0 No. 7337 passing Slade Reservoir with a Taunton to Ilfracombe train on 1st September, 1962. *P.W. Gray*

The south portals of Ilfracombe tunnels, photographed in October 1907.　　F.E. Box

1 in 36 down to Ilfracombe, the line passing through the twin-bore masonry and brick-lined tunnel 69½ yds in length." When the line was singled the original tunnel, that is the up one, was the tunnel that remained in use. Beyond the tunnel the Slade Reservoirs could be seen down in the valley.

Ilfracombe station (14 miles 74 ch.) was situated on a hill above the town and some 225 ft above sea level, its position causing nervous passengers to hope that the brakes would not fail and precipitate them down the slope. The gradient of 1 in 36 continued to the outer end of the platform where it eased to 1 in 71 and finally 1 in 353 as it approached the buffer stops. Shunting engines sometimes had to make several attempts before they could clear the points to switch stock from one road to another and no goods train was allowed to stand at the up advanced starter as it was on the gradient of 1 in 36. The terminal platform had two faces, but due to the position of the station building, the westerly one, Platform 2, was the longest and therefore the one normally used. By 1892 a screen on the off side of this platform road protected passengers from the prevailing west winds. This platform was provided with a run-round loop so at busy periods No. 2 was used for arrivals and No. 1 for departures. This custom started right at the beginning, for the working instructions issued for the opening of the line stated "As a general rule and invariably if possible, down trains will arrive at Ilfracombe on the left hand line as seen from a down train". The points of the run-round loop were worked from a ground frame. Before this loop was put in in 1929, gravity shunting was used to release engines of passenger trains and in February 1925 a coach ran through the buffers during this operation.

W.H. Smith opened a bookstall at the station early in August 1874. The platform was lengthened at some date (probably 1901 when some unstated improvements were made) prior to 1917 and an umbrella canopy added. On the west side of the station were three carriage sidings, another four being added in 1929 when the layout at Ilfracombe was altered and a new signal box provided which had 50 levers, of which 15 were spare. A track circuit was installed for 250 yds in the rear of the down outer home to the down inner home, the occupation of this stretch of line locking the down block commutator. To accommodate increasing holiday traffic, in April 1929 the station was again extended by a further 277 ft because for many years it had been inadequate for some trains, it being necessary to detrain passengers from the rear vehicles by means of steps on to the ballast. The opportunity was taken of raising the level of the old platform to the standard level of the new portion, the whole being paved with tarmac. The station buildings were reconditioned and improved, one advance being the installation of electric lighting. Col A.C. Trench inspected the revised layout on behalf of the Ministry of Transport on 9th May, 1929.

There was an interesting example of the use of double slip points to save length (the station was built on a man-made plateau) to give a direct run to all parts of the station. To the east of the passenger station was the random stone goods shed and four sidings. In 1926 the locomotive department employed a staff of ten which included four pairs of drivers and firemen. The original locomotive depot sited nearby had three engines shedded there on 31st December, 1922. Demolished by the Southern Railway, it was replaced to the south of the layout in July 1928 by a new single road through shed of pre-cast concrete, with a corrugated asbestos pitched roof. At the same time a 64 ft 10 in. turntable was installed nearby, later replaced by one of 70 ft to cater for Pacifics. The removal of the original engine shed gave room for the badly needed expansion of the goods depot. The whole site was a very difficult one to extend as the ground fell steeply from the station and yard for most of their perimeter and rose in a rock cutting on the remaining portion. Spoil taken out on the eastern side for lengthening

DESCRIPTION OF THE LINE

Ivatt class '2' 2-6-2T No. 41283 descends to Ilfracombe with a short freight, as the 12.25 to Taunton leaves on 27th July, 1963. *P.W. Gray*

Looking towards Mortehoe and Barnstaple from the end of Ilfracombe station on 23rd August, 1929. Note the stock in the head-shunt alongside the signal box and the complex point work. *R.W. Kidner*

An 'N' class 2-6-0 prepares to leave Ilfracombe No. 1 platform (*c.* 1950) while a tender first, smooth aired Pacific stands at No. 2 platform, with the carriage sidings in the background fairly well stocked. Note the goods shed and the yard crane. *M.E.J. Deane*

A view towards ilfracombe station showing the fine signal gantry alongside the single-road covered engine shed with 'N' class 2-6-0 No. 31842 at rest, on 23rd June, 1951.

T. Reardon

DESCRIPTION OF THE LINE 63

An 'M7' 0-4-4T at Ilfracombe *c.* 1935. GWR coaches can be seen to the left of the 'M7' on one of the extensive carriage sidings. *Lens of Sutton*

Ilfracombe, view up from the buffer stops in the 1950s. *Lens of Sutton*

64 THE BARNSTAPLE AND ILFRACOMBE RAILWAY

Excavating for the turntable pit, c. 1928. *Lens of Sutton*

The newly installed turntable in the summer of 1928. Note the amount of excavation required on this hillside site. *A. Hall*

the goods sidings and the new engine shed site was transferred to the west of the station to raise the ground for the extra carriage sidings. A small coal stage was provided for coaling engines by hand and an ash pit with a chute loading ashes into a wagon. The cleaner employed at the shed was laid off in the winter half of the year and had to find alternative employment. Because of the heavy traffic dealt with at the station during the summer, the extra staff came from various stations on the LSWR and stayed in lodgings. The turntable at Ilfracombe was exceptionally easy to rotate, so sometimes the wind would catch and revolve a locomotive or the "Devon Belle" observation car and the only way to stop it was to drop a sleeper in the pit. The turntable was removed on 26th October, 1964. Apart from Platform No. 1, the run-round loop and one carriage siding, all track at the station was taken out of use when the branch was singled on 17th December, 1967, a ground frame being installed in the shell of the signal box. The remaining carriage siding was taken out of use on 5th May, 1968. The former station area is now an industrial site.

View of Ilfracombe from the rear window of a departing 3-car Swindon Cross-Country dmu *circa* 1967. *D. Payne*

Ilfracombe station stood above the town in an extremely exposed position, a draught screen proved very desirable and here it is being erected. *Author's collection*

The draught screen and eight coach sidings can be seen in this view of 29th May, 1968.
A.E. West

Chapter Four

The Great Western Loop

In 1884 the GWR threatened to build an independent line from the D&S to Ilfracombe by-passing Barnstaple, causing the townsfolk to press the LSWR to make "a junction line between the two railways at Barnstaple in preference to the proposed new line". Scott consulted with Grierson resulting in the Bill being dropped and on 21st October, 1884 the LSWR agreed not to oppose the GWR Bill for a loop line, the two companies agreeing to the junction arrangements on 3rd July, 1885, the GWR undertaking to use no other route to Ilfracombe and being granted the use of Barnstaple Junction station for Ilfracombe traffic for an annual rental of £250 and a payment of 8 per cent on the cost of the extra accommodation provided.*

The line was built under the GWR Act of 31st July, 1885 which allowed a connecting line to be built from Victoria Road to Barnstaple Junction, this 1 mile 27 ch. of line being opened on 1st June, 1887 and allowing the Great Western to run through trains to Ilfracombe. It was stipulated that "The Through Carriages must be reserved for Passengers going to the Ilfracombe Branch, and Passengers for other Stations on the

A view looking south from the up end of Barnstaple station taken in September 1975 after closure of the Ilfracombe section. Behind the GWR pattern signals, in the distance at the foot of the hill, the embankments and viaduct of the loop line can be made out taking the railway to Barnstaple Victoria Road station. *R.W. Kidner*

---

* See Locomotion Papers No. 126 *The Taunton & Barnstaple Line* by the present author, for more details of the Devon & Somerset Railway.

L&SW must not be allowed to use them... but must ... proceed across the town to the LSWR Quay or Junction Stations as hitherto". These through railway coaches superseded the railway-owned coach service.

Leaving Victoria Road station with its timber buildings forming the terminus of the D&S line from Norton Fitzwarren, trains for Barnstaple Junction passed the engine shed and curved sharply south west on a single line rising at 1 in 117, and at the South Loop signal box, closed 12th June, 1960, joined a later East Curve which gave a direct run from Taunton to Barnstaple Junction avoiding Victoria Road Station. This curve opened on 1st July, 1905, and from 1925 onwards was generally open only from July to September. One or two coaches were usually detached from through down trains at the South Junction and hauled into Victoria Road by the shunting engine. In the other direction trains from Ilfracombe stopped at the East Junction to pick up coaches which had been propelled from Victoria Road. This East Curve closed on 4th September, 1939, was re-opened on 13th June, 1960 when Victoria Road was closed to passengers and all trains from Taunton used Barnstaple Junction, but Victoria Road remained open for goods traffic until 5th March, 1970. At the South Loop box the gradient steepened to 1 in 100 up, levelled out and then fell at 1 in 70. The line crossed the River Taw by a five span girder bridge. Its piers were constructed of 5 ft diameter wrought iron columns filled with concrete supporting two 85 ft long spans, two of 55 ft and one of 71½ ft. The spur joined the line from Exeter just south of Barnstaple Junction.

The turntable at Barnstaple Junction *circa* 1921. The passenger station is visible at the top left of the photograph. *Author's collection*

Chapter Five

Locomotives

LSWR and SR

Joseph Beattie foresaw that the Ilfracombe line would be difficult to work as it was built as a light railway and so required engines with a low axle loading and yet able to work trains over banks of two miles at 1 in 36 and three miles at 1 in 40, both on a sinuous formation, adding to the drawbar pull required. In 1870 he designed *Merlin*, a small 0-6-0 with 5ft 6in. coupled wheels, 14 ft wheelbase, 16 in. x 22 in. outside cylinders and a cut-down Lion class boiler. Not fully satisfied with his design, in February 1871 he asked Beyer, Peacock & Co. for advice, that firm proposed a mixed traffic inside-cylinder 4-4-0. The matter rested until the following February by which time Joseph had been succeeded by his son William George Beattie, who rejected the proposed 4-4-0 which would have been one of the first British classes with that wheel arrangement.

On 7th March, 1872 Beyer, Peacock & Co. quoted £2,800 for its standard light 0-6-0 with a four-wheeled tender. This resulted in a contract for supplying three of these engines being signed on 21st March. These locomotives were sold by the company to overseas railways with heavy gradients, notably Sweden. They had 4ft 6½in. coupled wheels, 13ft 10in. wheelbase, 16 in. x 20 in. cylinders and a total weight in working order of 35 tons 17½ cwt, the weight of 24 tons 7½ cwt on the driving wheels only just exceeding the 8 tons per axle restriction imposed on a Light Railway. The leading buffers were the padded leather type and all brake shoes were of wood, and in view of the steep gradients brakes were provided on the engine as well as the tender. These locomotives numbered 282/3/4 and were known as 'Ilfracombe Goods' engines, being delivered in February 1873 and run in initially from Nine Elms shed on goods and suburban passenger turns. By May Nos. 283 and 284 were working from Exeter and No. 282 on the Lymington branch, but for the opening of the Ilfracombe line they were transferred to Barnstaple. Their loads on passenger trains were restricted to not more than four vehicles with a brake van at each end and on goods trains they were restricted to a maximum load of eight wagons and a brake van.

In June 1874 Nos. 300 and 301 costing £2,790 each, were delivered and worked on the Lymington branch. No. 324 was delivered in April 1875. Nos. 393 and 394 were ordered by Beattie's successor William Adams in February 1880 at a cost of £2,900 apiece, the LSWR taking delivery in the

'Ilfracombe Goods' No. 394 pre-1903. The curved brass maker's plate is prominent over the centre wheel. *J.J. Hurd collection*

'A12' class Jubilee 0-4-2 at Ilfracombe, 8th November, 1907. *Phillipse*

autumn. This final pair had thicker tyres increasing the wheel diameter to 4ft 7½in., stovepipe chimneys, wrought iron spring buffers, larger sandboxes placed above the running plates and metal brake shoes. The weight of an engine and tender in working order was increased by almost a ton to 36 tons 14 cwt. In June 1881 the class was allocated: Nos. 282/3 Ilfracombe; Nos. 393/4 Barnstaple; Nos. 284, 324 Exeter; No. 301 Exmouth; No. 300 was under repair at Nine Elms Works, but normally shedded at Barnstaple. All the engines of the class were fitted with steam brakes and vacuum injectors replacing the hand brakes, as they visited the works between 1884 and 1887, while between March 1888 and September 1890 Adams rebuilt the first six engines making them similar to the last two of the class, and in 1890 all these engines were fitted with second-hand six-wheel tenders which replaced the original four-wheelers. Nos. 393 and 394 were not rebuilt, but supplied with six-wheel tenders in 1894 and 1891 respectively.

By the early nineteen-hundreds all had been supplanted on the Ilfracombe branch (an Adams 'A12' class *Jubilee* 0-4-2 was recorded at Ilfracombe on 8th November, 1907) and were withdrawn between 1905 and 1913, six having a further lease of life on light railways:

				Date Scrapped
No. 282	(later 0349) became Kent & East Sussex Railway	No. 7	*Rother*	10/38
No. 283	(later 0283) became Shropshire & Montgomeryshire Railway	No. 6	*Thisbe*	5/37
No. 284	(later 0284) became Kent & East Sussex Railway	No. 9	*Juno*	10/39
No. 300	(later 0300) became Shropshire & Montgomeryshire Railway	No. 5	*Pyramus*	3/32
No. 324	(later 0324) became Shropshire & Montgomeryshire Railway	No. 3	*Hesperus*	11/41
No. 394	(later 0394) became East Kent Railway	No. 3	—	3/35

Adams 'T1' 0-4-4 tank engines replaced the Ilfracombe goods engines and in 1907 those principally employed were Nos. 1, 2, 4, 69, 361, 363 and 367, the latter engine in September averaging only 23.8 lb. of coal per mile over the branch, the average consumption of the seven engines being 29. 7 lb. If unassisted, their load over the bank was restricted to 44 wheels. Around 1914 this class was replaced by 0-4-4 tank engines of the 'M7' class, No. 48 being noted in 1925 while in 1931 Nos. 36, 242, 250, 256 and 668 were shedded at Barnstaple Junction. Their duties on the branch later included being used as banking engines and pilots for the 'N' class. On summer Saturdays in the nineteen-thirties an 'M7' class 0-4-4 tank engine was stationed at Ilfracombe for use on pilot duties.

In the summer of 1925 'N' class 2-6-0s were first used on the branch. They were built to the original Maunsell design for the South Eastern &

'M7' class 0-4-4T No.699 at Braunton 28th July, 1936 heading a Bristol – Ilfracombe train comprising GWR coaches, with a Paddington – Illfracombe coach at the rear.

S. Miles Davey

'N' class No. A857 at Braunton ready to assist a down train. The 'A' stood for Ashford prefix it was eventually abandoned when South Eastern locomotives were renumbered by being given an additional 1000.

Author's collection

Chatham Railway by Woolwich Arsenal in 1920-2 to alleviate post-war unemployment; 20 were purchased by the SR in 1924 and a further 30 the following year. On 3rd March, 1925 No. A837 made a trial run from Queen Street, Exeter to Ilfracombe with 7 coaches, a tare weight of 204 tons. In the down direction the train ran through Braunton non-stop at 50 mph, but took 23 minutes to climb the 5¾ miles to Mortehoe, nearly stalling en route, finally arriving at Ilfracombe 43 minutes after leaving Barnstaple Junction. The next day from a standing start at Braunton it climbed to Mortehoe in 21¾ minutes achieving a speed of 12 mph on the 1 in 40 until reaching the curves just short of Mortehoe where the speed always fell.

In the up direction the 3¼ miles from Ilfracombe to Mortehoe were climbed in 16¾ minutes for the first trip, while on the second the engine reduced this to 14¾ minutes, but to achieve this figure had to be driven nearly flat out. To counteract the falling pressure the cut-off of 60 per cent was increased to 63 and 66 per cent while on the gradient of 1 in 36. The average time for up trips was just over 44½ minutes and 35½ minutes for the down trains. On 12th March comparative tests were made using an 'M7' class tank engine. No. E35 with six coaches, tare weight 122 tons, took 41 minutes on the down journey and then with a load of seven coaches, 150 tons, 43¾ minutes in the up direction.

Two very different types of mixed traffic locomotives at Barnstaple Junction on 21st July 1925: on the left a class 'A12' Jubilee 0-4-2, No. 628 and on the right 'N' class 2-6-0 N. 860.

H.C. Casserley

A local train headed by 'E/1R' class 0-6-2T No. B697 leaves Braunton for Ilfracombe one Sunday in August 1929. The 'E/1R' class was introduced in 1927 as a rebuild of the Stroudley 'E1' class 0-6-0T, a radial axle added to support the larger bunker required for passenger service in the West of England. *R.W. Kidner*

Conclusions were drawn that the 'M7s' were the most convenient locomotive for branch work, but that the 'N' class engines were better for working through trains from Exeter. Nos. A860 and 864 were noted on the line in 1925 working passenger, goods and banking turns.

The 'E1/R' class 0-6-2T, a rebuild by Maunsell of the Stroudley 'E1' class, mainly for the Torrington branch, sometimes worked light trains to Ilfracombe.

Engines of the 'King Arthur', 'Lord Nelson' and 'Schools' classes were too heavy for the branch, but the introduction of air-smoothed lightweight Pacifics of the 'West Country' and 'Battle of Britain' classes in 1945 and 1946 introduced a powerful engine within the weight limitations of the line. Eight of the 'West Country' class engines carried names of places on or near the branch:

34005 *Barnstaple*	34044 *Woolacombe*
34017 *Ilfracombe*	34046 *Braunton*
34029 *Lundy*	34093 *Saunton*
34043 *Combe Martin*	34094 *Mortehoe*

Engines of this class hauled most of the through passenger trains over the steeply-graded route and were also on banking duties, members of

LOCOMOTIVES

'West Country' Pacific No. 34024 *Tamar Valley* with the up "Atlantic Coast Express", 1st August, 1952
R.E. Toop

'Battle of Britain' class No. 34056 *Croydon* starts to cross the Taw viaduct with a down train, 1st August, 1952. Beyond the lady's head can just be seen a rival service, a Royal Blue coach carrying holiday passengers.
R.E. Toop

the 'N' class continuing to work local passenger and freight trains. When rebuilt, the Pacifics could not be used on the line as they were then too heavy. Seventeen minutes were allowed for the climb of six miles from Braunton to Mortehoe, almost four miles of this being at 1 in 40. If a 'West Country' was running late and had only three coaches, such as on a winter weekday, the distance could be covered in nine minutes, allowing the driver to make up no less than eight minutes on that section alone.

Ilfracombe to Exeter Central trains carried a headcode of a single lamp in front of the chimney, while a through train from Ilfracombe to Taunton carried a lamp above each buffer.

LIST OF LOCOMOTIVES SHEDDED AT BARNSTAPLE AND ILFRACOMBE (Ilfracombe was a sub shed of Barnstaple.)

Barnstaple was allotted the BR Code 72E, recoded 83F in December 1962 when the shed came under Western Region control.

JUNE 1933

'M7' class 0-4-4T	'E1/R' class 0-6-2T	'N' class 2-6-0
36	2094	1829
242	2095	1833
250	2124	1850
256	2608	1856
377		2610
668		2696
		2697

Total 17 locomotives

JANUARY 1947

'M7' class 0-4-4T	'E1/R' class 0-6-2T
23	2094
36	2095
42	2096
44	2608
247	2610
250	2696
321	
670	

Total 14 locomotives

MAY 1959

'M7' class 0-4-4T	Class '2' 2-6-2T
30247	41294
30251	41295
30253	41297
30254	41298
30255	41314
30256	
30671	

Total 12 locomotives

After Nationalisation, LMSR Ivatt 2-6-2 tank engines were used if there was a shortage of 'N' class locomotives, sometimes these tank engines being used as bankers. Eventually they replaced all the duties of the 'M7s'. Occasionally, a BR Standard Class 4MT 2-6-4 tank engine would replace a failed 'N' class engine and 0-6-2 tank engines of the 'E1/R' class sometimes appeared.

The final day of regular steam working was 5th September, 1964, also the last day the "Atlantic Coast Express" ran. From then on trains were

Ivatt class '2' 2-6-2T No. 41298 and '43XX' class 2-6-0 No. 7337 near Heddon Mill with the 07.00 Taunton to Ilfracombe on 27th July, 1963.   *P.W. Gray*

Diesel hydraulic, 'Warship' No. D817 *Foxhound* heads the 18.20 Ilfracombe to Exeter St David's, the return working of a through Paddington to Ilfracombe train on 27th July, 1968. The water column that used to sit on the end of the platform at Braunton has been removed and the former down line lifted. A 15 mph speed restriction has been imposed on the former crossover. *R.A. Lumber*

'Hymek' diesel hydraulic No. 7097 enters Barnstaple Junction with a down train in August 1965. *D. Payne*

diesel multiple units, though locomotives, usually Type 4 'Warships' being the most popular, appeared with the through trains on summer Saturdays. Class 70XX diesel-hydraulics also appeared but were limited to a maximum load of 280 tons.

Dugald Drummond's 'F9' class inspection saloon, nicknamed "The Bug" really a 4-2-4 tank engine with a short saloon on the rear bogie, traversed the branch and on one occasion its wheels slipped on the wet rails as the brakes were applied on the descent to Ilfracombe, control was lost and the engine struck the buffer stops. To prevent a recurrence, on the next visit of "The Bug" to Ilfracombe a vacuum braked coach was coupled to its rear nearly causing it to stall on the 1 in 40 climb from Braunton.

GWR

In the early days Great Western through trains were hauled by LSWR locomotives between Barnstaple and Ilfracombe, though by 1917 GWR engines were working them. During the First World War a GWR outside frame 4-4-0 was parked in Ilfracombe yard for several days. Great Western engines working through trains over the line were usually 2-6-0s of the '43XX' etc. class, Moguls shedded at Taunton having their steps cut down to 8ft 4in. for operating over the Ilfracombe branch. The

A GWR '4575' class 2-6-2T at Barnstaple Town om a Taunton – Ilfracombe working in 1934. It connected with the narrow gauge train to Lynton seen on the far left. Although common on this line, it was generally unusual for tank engines, as opposed to tender engines, to work over another company's line. *F.E. Box*

'Bulldog' class 4-4-0 No. 3348 *Launceston* with a combined number and nameplate and 'M7' class 0-4-4T No. 25 climb the 1 in 36 vank *circa* 1927. *A. Halls*

small 2-6-2T class was also used. One observer watched the "Atlantic Coast Express" with a Pacific fore and aft leave Ilfracombe with much slipping, while a GWR Mogul with a Wolverhampton train made up to a similar load departed without slipping and with such acceleration that its 'N' class banker was left behind only to catch it up on the 1 in 36 bank. Latterly when the branch came into Western Region territory, an 0-6-0 of the 2251 class appeared on the line replacing a failed 'N' class. In order to make more economic use of locomotives and crews and to give route knowledge in the event of a diversion having to be made due to enemy activity, in May 1942 Exmouth Junction 'T9' 4-4-0s worked between Exeter and Yeovil via Taunton and Martock. To balance this mileage, GWR '43XX' class 2-6-0s worked from Exeter Central to Barnstaple and Ilfracombe.

Locomotives of the following classes were allowed to run between Barnstaple and Ilfracombe:
SR: N; NI; U; U1; E1/R; B4; C14; G6; L12; M7; 02: Q; Q1; S11; T9; 'West Country'; 'Battle of Britain'; 0395; 757; 0415; 0298; 700; 0458.
BR Class 2 2-6-0; Class 4 2-6-0.
LMSR Class 2 2-6-2T; Class 4 2-6-0; Class 4 2-6-4T.
WR (1960) 45XX; 55XX; 22XX; 32XX; 43XX; 53XX; 63XX; 73XX.
WR locomotives were required to have their steps cut back to a width of 8 ft 4 in. if lower than 1 ft 9 in. above rail level.

Chapter Six

Rolling Stock

Four-wheeled coaches were used in the early years, and six-wheelers by the 'eighties. After 1900 corridor stock of the high-roofed type appeared on the through trains, and continued in use until after 1930. Meanwhile short high-roofed and low-roofed bogie stock in 2 and 3-coach sets handled the local workings. In 1926 ten 3-coach Maunsell corridor sets were built for the West of England services; these had very large luggage brake compartments (each brake coach in the set had only 4 passenger compartments); this was no doubt due to the amount of luggage holiday-makers then took with them. These were sets 390-399. Four more sets (445-8) came out in 1927. There were also a number of loose brake-composites, required in winter-time when only one coach on the "Atlantic Coast Express" went through to any one destination. The former LSWR corridor stock was gradually phased out as the Maunsell stock came in; in the summer there was sometimes a shortage of local stock and ex-LBSC carriages were used on occasion.

The two observation cars for the rear of the "Devon Belle" were converted by the Pullman Car Company at its Preston Park Works from 'J' class cars Nos. 13 and 14 of 1921, both of which had been rebuilt with

The observation car of the "Devon Belle" in 1952, the train being banked in the rear by an 'N' class 2-6-0. *N. Wellings*

kitchens in 1937. When in service on the "Devon Belle" they had steel underframes, 59 ft wooden bodies and weighed 33 tons. The cars were equipped with a bar, pantry, lavatory and observation saloon for 27 passengers in single and double tub seats available to both first and third class passengers. The observation cars necessarily had to be turned at Ilfracombe and London so that the observation end windows remained at the back of the train. After the cessation of the "Devon Belle", the two observation cars were painted Midland lake and one used on the North Wales Land Cruise train "The Welsh Chieftain". The other was utilised on the Inverness to Kyle of Lochalsh line until 1967 when it was transferred to the Glasgow to Oban route, being withdrawn from BR service in 1968. No. 13 is now on the Dart Valley Railway in South Devon.

Before the First World War, during the summer the "Torbay Express" had a slip coach portion for Ilfracombe and this was probably the only slip portion in history to include a restaurant car in its four-coach formation.

The 1936 GWR Rule Book stated that 60 ft by 9 ft were the maximum dimensions of Great Western coaches allowed over the Ilfracombe line and that no coaches with lower centre-step boards would be accepted. The SR agreed to the running of London & North Eastern Railway coaching stock 59 ft long (63ft 7 in. over buffers) and 9 ft width.

In 1954 the 3.00 pm ex-Waterloo conveyed a restaurant car to Ilfracombe, though it was only advertised as running as far as Exeter, the vehicle returning on the 10.30 am from Ilfracombe the following morning. 1955 saw the appearance of the only BR Standard triple restaurant car set S9, S1006 and S80009 on the Saturdays only midday train from Waterloo to Ilfracombe which returned at 10.00 am the following day, then normally remained unused until the following Saturday. The midday train from Ilfracombe on Saturdays conveyed the restaurant car from the previous day's 3.00 pm ex-Waterloo. During the peak holiday season, the Friday "Atlantic Coast Express", instead of taking the restaurant car to Padstow, hauled it to Ilfracombe, it returning on the 10.30 the following morning.

LMS coaches with lower centre footboards were prohibited from working over the line, while lateral clearances on many of the tight curves were insufficient to accommodate the 'swing' of a GWR 70 ft coach, so when the "Cornish Riviera Express" was composed of 70 ft stock, the exception was the 60 footer for Ilfracombe. GWR 'B' sets worked through from Taunton to Ilfracombe.

Chapter Seven

Permanent Way and Signalling

As previously stated the line was built as a light railway with about 5¾ miles of 60 lb./yd flat-bottomed rail in 24 ft lengths fixed directly to the sleepers by fang bolts inside and spikes outside, while there were three miles of 72⅛ lb./yd rails in five and six metre lengths fished at the joints with only three bolts as was the French custom, suggesting that the rail was originally intended for France. The six miles of heavy gradients, that is from Heddon Mill Crossing to Mortehoe and Mortehoe to Ilfracombe, were laid with 75 lb./yd LSWR standard double-headed rail in 24 ft lengths set in 32 lb. chairs. Over the iron bridge at Barnstaple bullhead rail was used. When the line was first opened no check rails were provided on the sharp curves, the sharpest of which had a radius

SIGNAL BOXES, CROSSOVER ROADS AND CATCH POINTS.

* Signal box provided with closing switch.   † Catch points worked from signal box.
Block instruments in booking office.   Crossover road worked from ground frame.
¶ Unworked trailing points.

Station and signal boxes.	Distance from next box, above. Mls. yds.	Position of box (in regard to station).	Crossover roads. Position (in regard to signal box), or description.	Yards from box.	Catch points exist in Line.	Yards from box.	Gradient rising 1 in
Barnstaple Jct.							
East (To G.W.R.	4 434 1 286)	Up side (Chapelton end)	Chapelton side	78	Middle	286† (Barnstaple Town side)	651
West (To Fremington	— 359 2 958)	In fork of junction	—	—	Middle	73† (Chapelton side)	651
Barnstaple Town							
Station	— 957	Platform	—	—	—	—	—
Pottington	— 642	Down side (Wrafton side)	Wrafton side	369¶			
Wrafton							
Station*	4 89	Down platform	Barnstaple side	202	—	—	—
Braunton							
Station	— 1,623	Down platform	Wrafton side Mortehoe side	187 95	—	—	—
Heddon Mill Crossing*	2 394	Up side (Mortehoe side)	—	—	Down	352 (Braunton side)	83
Mortehoe							
Station	3 1,058	Down platform	Braunton side Ilfracombe side	124 168	Down Up	574 (Braunton side) 482 (Ilfracombe side)	40 76
Ilfracombe							
Station	2 1,604	Down side (Mortehoe side)	Mortehoe side Station side	51 31	—	—	—

From Southern Railway Working Timetable Appendices (Western Section) 1934.

of 7½ chains, but following a derailment on 24th December, 1889, the Board of Trade inspector recommended that they be fitted. Ballast was broken stone and hard shale while the fencing was wooden post and rail. The doubled line was laid with LSWR standard permanent way. To cope with runaways on the severe gradients, catch points were situated between Braunton and Heddon Mill Crossing; Heddon Mill Crossing and Mortehoe; Mortehoe and Ilfracombe. The Great Western loop line at Barnstaple was originally laid with a 76 lb./yd bullhead rail in 36 lb. chairs.

The *Western Morning News* describing the line in 1874 announced with awe that the branch was equipped with Saxby & Farmer's block signalling system. The 1874 working timetables stated that trains on the branch were worked under the Staff and Ticket system as well as Absolute Single Line Block Regulations. Latterly the standard electric token was used on the single line between Barnstaple Junction and Barnstaple Town, while between the Town station and Pottington signal box a non-returnable electric token was employed. Braunton signal box locked the crossing gates at both ends of the station, as well as those at Georgeham Crossing half a mile to the north.

Name of Box	No. of Working Levers	No. of Spare Levers
1889		
Barnstaple Junction	42	4
1890		
Raleigh Cabinet Works (level crossing)	?	?
Barnstaple Quay	?	?
Pottington (swing bridge)	17	2
Pottington (level crossing)	6	0
Duckpool (Chivenor) (level crossing)	5	3
Wrafton (station and level crossing)	15	2
Vellator (level crossing)	5	2
Braunton (level crossing)	2	3
Braunton (station and level crossing)	21	3
New signal boxes built when Braunton to Ilfracombe line was doubled:		
Georgeham (level crossing)	3	2
Stoney Bridge (level crossing)	5	1
Heddon Mill (level crossing)	8	0
Mortehoe (station)	16	4
Ilfracombe (station)	50	10*

* Provision was made for adding 2 more platform roads at a future date.

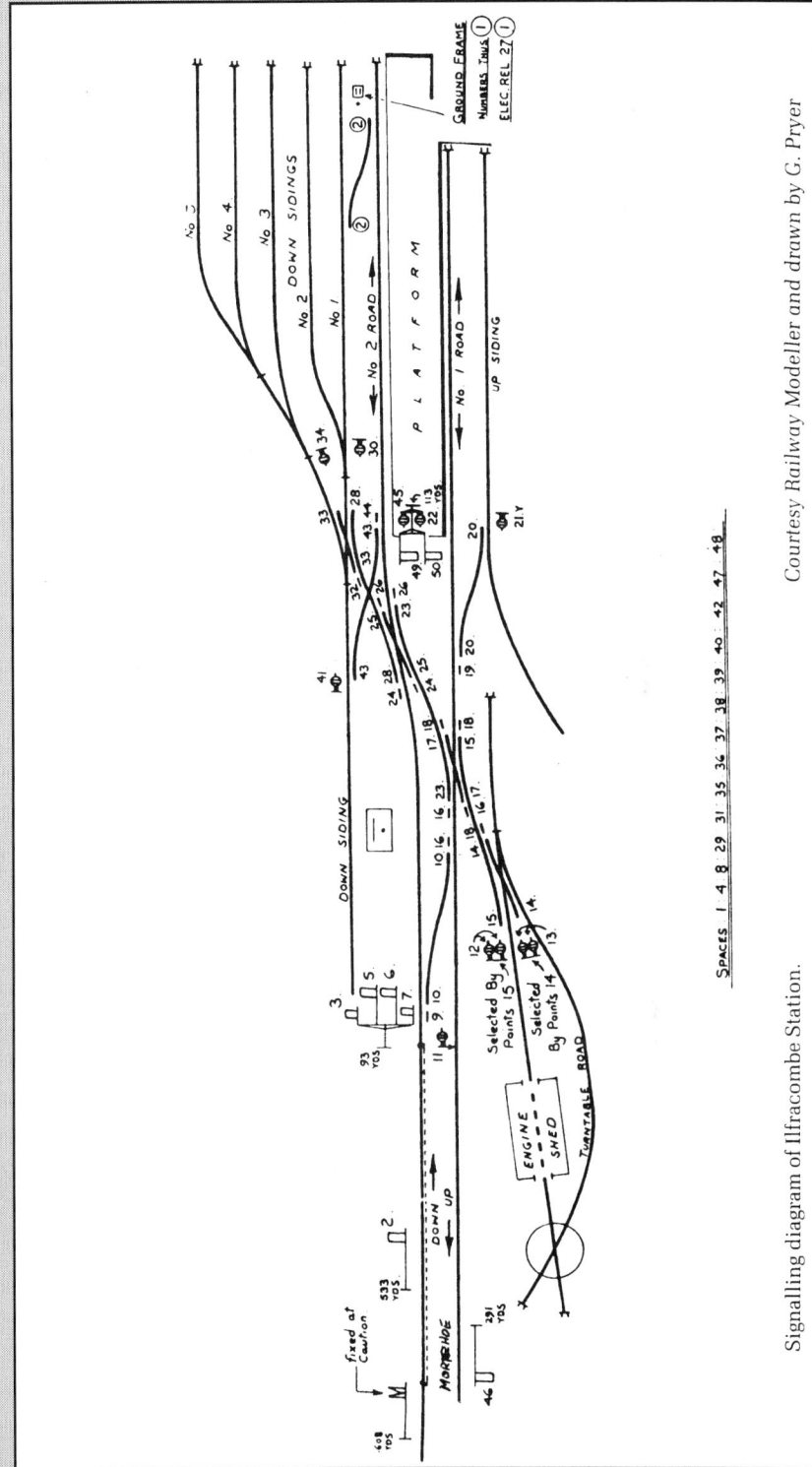

Signalling diagram of Ilfracombe Station.

Courtesy Railway Modeller and drawn by G. Pryer

Ilfracombe station staff gather to celebrate Tom Short's last load, 21st November 1908. Van man Tom Short stands on the LSWR horse-drawn parcels delivery van.

S. Hatchley collection

Permanent and summer staff of Illfracombe station, 1928. *S. Hatchley collection*

Chapter Eight

Passenger and Freight Services

Passenger Services

In LSWR days the principal North Devon line was that which ran from Coleford Junction to Bideford and Torrington, the section from Barnstaple Junction to Ilfracombe being worked as the branch. In Southern Railway days the latter took over as the more important route for passenger services but on the freight side the traditional pattern continued to the end.

When the line was opened between Ilfracombe and Barnstaple five down and four up passenger trains were provided on weekdays only, up trains being allowed 48 minutes for the distance of 15 miles and down trains 55 minutes. Four up trains connected with expresses to Waterloo, the fastest times being 7 h 52 m up and 7 h 18 m down for the distance of 226½ miles. The Devon & Somerset Railway's fastest competitive rail and coach service to and from Paddington was 7½ hours in either direction. In August the timetable was amended to give an extra up train, making five each way, two in each direction omitting to stop at Wrafton. By August 1880 six trains were running in each direction and the service was faster, down trains taking an average of 48 and up trains 44 minutes. In August 1887, six up trains ran daily plus an extra on Mondays,

An 11 coach down train at Pines Dean between Braunton and Mortehoe. 'M7' class 0-4-4T No. 322 pilots the 2-6-0 train engine, while another 0-4-4T acts as rear banker. *A. Hall*

Wednesdays, Fridays and Saturdays with seven in the reverse direction. The fastest trains between Ilfracombe and Waterloo took 7 h 10 m up and 6 h 32 m down; the fastest Great Western trains serving Paddington took 7 h 50 m and 7 h 15 m respectively for the distance of 224¾ miles. The solitary Parliamentary train by this route took no less than 12 h 6 m and landed passengers in the capital at 4.00 am.

From 1st July, 1889 N.J. Burlinson, the new GWR superintendent of the line, improved the service to Ilfracombe. The "Ilfracombe Express" covered the journey from Paddington in 6 h 55 m while through coaches off the "Zulu" did the journey even faster – in 6 h 2 m compared with the quickest LSWR express which took 6 h 22 m. The "Liverpool Express" made the journey to Ilfracombe in 10 h 47 m, the corresponding train in the reverse direction taking 9 h 55 m. The Midland Railway advertised through coaches from Bradford to Ilfracombe via the Somerset & Dorset Railway and LSWR. By December of that year an additional up train had been put on between Ilfracombe and Barnstaple.

The first Sunday train service began on 1st June, 1890 when one ran each way. In July complaints were received regarding the late arrival of trains. Passengers who should have arrived at Ilfracombe at 9.08 pm on Saturday evening did not reach there until the early hours of Sunday morning. Trains from the north were also delayed. Accommodation at the station was inadequate and it took nearly an hour to clear a crowded train of passengers and luggage which meant that the next came in before the operation was

'43XX' class 2-6-0 on through GWR down train on 5th August, 1932 at Barnstaple Town station. A Lynton and Barnstaple locomotive stands on the left. *F.E. Box*

complete, thus adding to the confusion. It was thought that when the GWR obtained running powers to Ilfracombe in 1887, improvements should have been made to the station.

In July 1891 eight down and nine up trains ran on weekdays between Barnstaple and Ilfracombe, with one up train on Sunday evening. Most down trains were scheduled to cover the distance in 47 and up trains in 44 minutes, although one down train omitting stops at Wrafton and Braunton took only 39, the corresponding up train taking 36 minutes. LSWR and GW trains from London took about the same time, the fastest services leaving Waterloo and Paddington simultaneously at 3.00 pm (the GW train being the "Zulu") and arriving at Ilfracombe at 9.08 pm. The fastest up trains took 5 h 50 m to Waterloo and 6 h 10 m to Paddington, the Great Western service generally being a little slower than that of the LSWR. In July 1891 through coaches were run in both directions between Ilfracombe, Liverpool and Manchester.

During the early part of the 20th century the service continued to improve. July 1904 saw eleven down and thirteen up trains with one up service on Sundays. The following summer a further increase took place, thirteen down and fifteen up trains running, including a luncheon corridor train in 5 h 35 m from and 5 h 15 m to Waterloo. On Sundays the service increased to three down and two up trains. The timetable for July 1906 showed fifteen down and sixteen up with two each way on Sundays. On 2nd June, 1906 the Great Western had opened its shorter line to the west via Frome and this reduced the mileage from Paddington to 203¾ against the previous 224¾, making it 22¾ miles shorter than the LSWR route and allowing the Paddington to Ilfracombe time to be reduced to 4 h 55 m compared with 5 h 13 m from Waterloo, but keen competition for the West of England traffic was ended by a pooling agreement signed in May 1910.

As one method of increasing traffic the LSWR issued circular tour tickets incorporating a trip on the Ilfracombe line. One example available in 1908 was London-Ilfracombe-Bideford by rail, then road coach to Clovelly, Bude, Boscastle and Camelford, to Wadebridge by rail, on to Newquay by coach and return to London via Wadebridge and the North Cornwall line, all for £2 16s. 8d., third class.

In the summer of 1909 the seventeen down trains from Barnstaple included one which left Waterloo at 11.10 and was the forerunner of the "Atlantic Coast Express" and took 5 h 13 m to arrive at Ilfracombe, the second through train taking 5 h 17 m. The up service at this time totalled seventeen trains and four down and three up ran on Sundays. In April 1910 ten trains ran in each direction, stopping at all stations between Barnstaple Junction and Ilfracombe except for two each way which omitted Wrafton.

BARNSTAPLE JUNCTION.

Saw Milling and General Supplies siding.—The Company's engine will place the wagon, or wagons, just outside (i.e., on the siding side) of the gate defining the Company's boundary, and the trader will provide staff to receive such wagon or wagons. The trader's staff will be responsible for the application of the brakes and scotches necessary to keep the wagons at rest, and the only duty devolving upon the Company's Shunter is to uncouple the engine from the wagons.

In the event of the trader's staff not being present to accept the transfer, the wagon or wagons must be brought back to the station.

In like manner wagons from the siding will be brought to the gate by the trader's staff who will be responsible for efficiently braking and scotching the vehicles so that the Company's engine may be coupled to them. The time of transfer to or from the siding to be mutually arranged between the Barnstaple Junction Station Master and the District Manager of the Saw Milling and General Supplies Company.

Under no circumstances should any of the Company's staff manipulate brakes, scotches, or perform any act in connection with the braking of vehicles beyond the gate defining the Company's boundary in connection with this siding.

The curvature of this siding is about 3 chains, consequently it must not be used by six-wheeled vehicles and great care must be exercised when bogie vehicles are being moved into or out of the siding to prevent them becoming buffer-locked.

Shapland and Petter's siding.—Vehicles for the siding must be propelled from Barnstaple Junction by an engine, with a brake van as the leading vehicle. On arrival at the siding the brake van is to be detached and left on the running line. The van brake must be securely applied by the person in charge before shunting operations are commenced.

The Company's engine must not proceed into the siding beyond the boundary gate, at which point ingoing and outgoing wagons must be exchanged.

On completion of the work at the siding, the engine must haul the vehicles to Barnstaple Junction with the brake van at the rear.

BETWEEN BARNSTAPLE TOWN AND BARNSTAPLE JUNCTION.

In connection with the propelling movement with the empty van of the down morning mail train, the Guard must ride in the van and hand signal the movement throughout, keeping a sharp look-out for fixed signals.

The Enginemen must also be alert, obey fixed signals, and act promptly upon the hand signals exhibited by the Guard.

The engine whistle must be sounded on approaching each of the level crossings between Barnstaple Town and Barnstaple Junction stations.

MORTEHOE.

An up goods train doing work at this station must have the rear portion propelled across to the down line by way of the crossover road at the Braunton end, so that the rear brake van may be available to hold wagons during the formation of the train. When the work of such train is complete it should be started away from the down line by way of the same crossover road under control of the ground signal applicable thereto.

During shunting operations in connection with a down goods train, the rear portion must be shunted into the down sidings and not allowed to stand upon the running line.

BETWEEN BRAUNTON AND ILFRACOMBE.

Working over Inclines.—The gradients of the line between Braunton and Ilfracombe are as follow :—

Between mile posts.	Gradient rising towards Ilfracombe.	Between mile posts.	Gradient falling towards Ilfracombe.
217 and 217½	1 in 132, 236 and 74	223¼ and 223½	1 in 190 and 76
217½ and 218	1 in 74 and 96	223½ and 223¾	1 in 76, 133, 445 and 1320
218 and 218¾	1 in 96, 87, 128 and 82	223¾ and 224	1 in 1320, 68 and 36
218¾ and 219¼	1 in 82, 73 and 83	224 and 226	1 in 36
219¼ and 219½	1 in 83, 190 and 100	226 and termination	1 in 36, 71 and 353
219½ and 220¾	1 in 100, 50 and 40		
220¾ and 221	1 in 40, 388 and 100		
221 and 222¾	1 in 41, 45 and 40		
222¾ and 223	1 in 40		
223 and 223¼	1 in 40 and 288		

The following is a list of self-acting catch points :—

Line.	Situated between	Gradient rising.
Down	Braunton and Heddon Mill crossing, 352 yards from Heddon Mill crossing box	1 in 83.
Down	Heddon Mill crossing and Mortehoe, 574 yards from Mortehoe signal box	1 in 40.
Up	Between Ilfracombe and Mortehoe, 482 yards from Mortehoe signal box	1 in 76.

Passenger trains.—The maximum loads of S.R. passenger trains, worked by one engine, from Braunton to Mortehoe and from Ilfracombe to Mortehoe, are as under :—

When worked by " Drummond " tank engine	140 tons.
When worked by " N " class engine	180 tons.

The maximum loads of trains worked by G.W.R. engines are as follows :—

2—6—0 Class No. 43	190 tons or 8 coaches of 24 tons each.
$\frac{2-6-2}{T}$ Class No. 45	170 tons or 7 coaches of 24 tons each.
4—4—0 " Bulldog " class ..	145 tons or 6 coaches of 24 tons each.
0—6—0 Standard goods class ..	120 tons or 5 coaches of 24 tons each.

Passenger trains exceeding the weight shown must have an assisting engine attached. The assisting engine may be attached at the front of the train provided the load does not exceed 280 tons. If, however, the load exceeds 280 tons, the assisting engine must be attached at the rear of the train from Braunton to Mortehoe, or Ilfracombe to Mortehoe, as the case may be.

If a Driver finds it necessary to request the provision of an assisting engine with less than the load laid down for one engine, he must report the matter to his Foreman on completion of his duty, stating the cause.

No passenger train must consist of more than 88 wheels.

All passenger trains between Braunton and Ilfracombe must have hand brake fitted vehicles attached as follows :—

Not exceeding 180 tons : 1 bogie vehicle with brake compartment. This vehicle to be included in the total tonnage.

Exceeding 180 tons : 2 bogie vehicles with brake compartments, 1 of which must be marshalled at the rear. These vehicles to be included in the total tonnage.

A Guard must travel in the rear brake vehicle when the load exceeds 180 tons.

A vehicle with a brake compartment must be provided at the rear of vehicles conveying passengers from Braunton to Mortehoe, or Ilfracombe to Mortehoe, as the case may be, except when an assisting engine is attached at the rear of the train.

Two horse boxes, carriage trucks, vans or other similar vehicles, may be attached outside the rear vehicle with a brake compartment, provided they are fitted with the vacuum brake complete, in good working order, and are also provided with a hand brake.

In no circumstances must a vehicle, fitted with a vacuum pipe only, be placed at the rear of a train.

Should the vacuum brake power of a train become inoperative from any cause, care must be taken to reduce the load so that the train may be safely controlled on any part of the inclines with the hand brake power available.

Goods trains.—The maximum loads of goods trains from Braunton to Mortehoe or from Ilfracombe to Mortehoe are as follows :—

Train worked by one engine .. ..
- " Drummond " tank engine—equal to 11 loaded goods vehicles, including van.
- " N " class engine—equal to 15 loaded goods vehicles, including van.

Train worked by more than one engine : equal to 25 vehicles, inclusive of vans.

When an assisting engine is attached it must be placed at the rear of the train.

A goods train from Mortehoe to Ilfracombe or from Mortehoe to Braunton must not exceed a load equal to 25 loaded goods vehicles, including brake vans.

A goods train worked by one engine only must have brake vans attached, with a man in each, as follows :

Not exceeding a load equal to 11 loaded goods vehicles	1 van
Above 11 and not exceeding 15 loaded goods vehicles	2 ten-ton vans or one 20-ton van
Above 15 and not exceeding 25 loaded goods vehicles	1 ten-ton van and one 20-ton van

The loads shown are inclusive of brake vans.

When two brake vans are attached, the 20-ton van must be placed at the rear of the train, and the other behind the eleventh vehicle of the train.

When two engines are attached, both engines must be at the front of the train, and one 20-ton brake van only need be provided.

Should the climatic conditions render the rails unfavourable for the prompt stoppage of trains, a sufficient number of wagon brakes should be securely applied to counteract this before leaving Mortehoe. Drivers and Guards must communicate with one another with respect to this duty, and they will be held responsible for any neglect of this order.

In calculating the number of vehicles, this must be done in accordance with the table shown in the Working Timetable.

Should any vehicles fitted with the automatic vacuum brake be attached, they must, as far as practicable, be attached next the engine and the vacuum brake connected up, in which case they need not be included when calculating the number of brake vans required.

A ballast train consisting of bogie hopper wagons fitted with the vacuum brake throughout, in working order, must be operated in accordance with the instructions applicable to passenger trains, with the exception that the load must not exceed six loaded bogie hopper wagons and two brake vans.

ILFRACOMBE

The shunting of coaching stock by means of gravitation on the incline at Ilfracombe station is strictly prohibited.

Goods vehicles must not be drawn on to the incline on the running line during shunting operations, unless such a course is absolutely necessary. When this arrangement must, of necessity, be resorted to, a braked vehicle must be attached at the station end of the wagons and a man provided to ride on such vehicle and apply the brake in case of emergency.

CARRIAGE WORKINGS, ILFRACOMBE
WEEK DAYS, Commencing Monday 21st September, 1931, and until further notice.
(Workings of Loose Stock not included.)

Train	Destination	Formation	Wkg. No.	Previous Service Train	From	Due
am				am		am
Berth ... —		1 cor.bke compo 1 bogie van	—	1.30	Waterloo ...	7.35
8.15	Waterloo ...	1 cor.bke cpo	—	—	Berth ...	—
9.00	Exeter, thence 11.21 to Salisbury	3 lav. set	247	—	Berth ...	—
9.55	Paddington **A** ...	1 GW coach	—	—	Berth ...	—
	Barnstaple Jn ...	2-set ...	163	7.25	Barnstaple Jn ...	8.13
10.25	Waterloo ...	1 cor.bke cpo	—	—	Berth ...	—
pm						
12.17	Waterloo ...	2 (?) cor.bke compos	—	—	Berth ...	—
1.40	Taunton **A** ...	GWR stock	—	—	Berth ...	—
2.00	Waterloo ...	2 cor.brake compos	—	—	Berth ...	—
3.00	Exeter ...	3 cor.set (G)	39	6.25	Yeovil Town ...	10.46 pm
Berth ... —		1 cor.bke cpo	—	8.40	Waterloo ...	3.31
Berth ... —		1 cor.bke cpo 1 GW coach	—	11.00 —	Waterloo ... Paddington **B** ...	4.27 am
4.45	Exeter ...	3 cor.set (G)	42	9.42 pm	Exeter ...	11.57 pm
6.10	Barnstaple Jn ...	2-set ...	163	5.15	Barnstaple Jn ...	6.00
Berth ... —		GWR stock	—	—	Paddington **B** ...	6.55
Berth ... —		2 cor. brake compos	—	12.40	Waterloo ...	7.22
7.35	Exeter ...	2 lav. set	200	1.44 am	Yeoford ...	3.31
		3 cor.set (G)	40	11.48 pm	Exeter ...	2.09
Berth ... —		3 lav. set 1 cor.bke cpo	246 —	6.30 3.00	Exeter ... Waterloo ...	8.28

NOTES:
A Worked by SR engine Ilfracombe to Barnstaple Junction.
B Worked by SR engine Barnstaple Junction to Ilfracombe.

SET TRAINS:
3 corridor sets, Type G. Nos. 403/6/7/12/4/5/7–22.
   Formation: Third brake (4-compt.); Compo (4 1sts 3 3rds); Third brake (4 compt.). Ex-L & SWR.
     2-sets (non-lavatory). Nos. 34—41/3/5—55, 375.   Ex-L & SWR
     2-sets (lavatory). Nos. 1–21.   Ex-L & SWR
     3-sets (lavatory). Nos. 56–86, 95–9, 173–8.   Ex-L & SWR
     Corridor brake compos (loose stock).   SR

Down trains took 44 minutes and up trains 39. The LSWR "North Devon & Ilfracombe Corridor Express" having a luncheon car to Exeter, left Waterloo at 11.00 am, arriving at Ilfracombe 5 h 23 m later at 4.23 pm. The up "London Corridor Express" with a luncheon car from Exeter to Waterloo, left Ilfracombe at 11.00 am and arrived at Waterloo at 4.40 pm giving a time of 5 h 40 m. The fastest times by GWR were 5 h 53 m down and 6 h up. That summer the Great Central Railway inaugurated a train from Leeds Central to Ilfracombe via Oxford.

In the timetable for October 1913 to June 1914 nine trains each way were run, taking about 40 minutes for the journey between Barnstaple Junction and Ilfracombe, with two each way on Sundays. The 1914 summer timetable showed an additional four trains each way on weekdays and one extra one on Sundays. On summer afternoons a train ran from Ilfracombe to Mortehoe and returned in the evening. That winter there were nine weekday and two Sunday trains each way.

The next 25 years which saw the First World War and the amalgamation by the Southern Railway, also witnessed the branch gain in importance, particularly for holiday traffic. Through restaurant car trains on weekdays during the 1930 Summer service included the 10.40 am, and 12.00 noon (FSO) from Waterloo, and the 7.40 am (MO), 10.25 am ACE, and 11.15 am (SO) from Ilfracombe. The seventeen trains from Barnstaple Junction to Ilfracombe on Mondays to Fridays in the summer of 1938 included six from Waterloo, of which the newspaper train from London at 1.30 am took passengers only from Salisbury. This situation, changed after the Second

'N' class 2-6-0 No. 1409 with an up train, at Barnstaple Junction, on 18th July, 1935. The engine shed is to the right of the smoke box and the goods shed can be seen beyond the coaches.

S.W. Baker

THE BARNSTAPLE AND ILFRACOMBE RAILWAY

Bradshaw April 1910 Passenger Timetable.

1953 respectively. The first train from Yeovil followed at 10.59 am and then at 11.18 am the 8.30 am from Taunton, instituted in 1950. The second Yeovil service reached Ilfracombe at 12.11 pm, and the first Waterloo service which had left at 7.40 am came in at 1.39 pm (later 7.38 am, arriving 1.27 pm). This was followed at 2.05 pm by the 11.39 am all stations from Exeter Central which in 1962 was diverted to run to Plymouth instead of Ilfracombe. Waterloo services then came in at 2.21 pm (8.27 am, later 8.22 am from London), 2.40 pm (8.35 am from London) and 3.22 pm (8.47 am, later 8.54 am). The 8.22 am from Waterloo was the first to be withdrawn, having disappeared from the timetable by 1962, the 8.54 am following in 1963.

The next train was the 10.05 am from Waterloo introduced in 1949 and amended to 10.15 am in 1953, which arrived at 3.40 pm. Like the 8.35 am from Waterloo this was a through working from Salisbury for a light Pacific from that shed. A 12.50 pm from Taunton arrived at 3.56 pm and was followed by the main portion of the "Atlantic Coast Express" at 4.10 pm, the 10.35 am from Waterloo. Later changes to this train are detailed in another section. The 11.30 am through train from Paddington arrived at 5.11 pm and ran until 1962. In 1963 it started from Taunton and arrived at 4.53 pm, but disappeared altogether in 1964. The 12.00 noon Waterloo-Ilfracombe "Devon Belle" arrived at 5.27 pm until 1954 after which it was replaced by a train of ordinary stock which left Waterloo at 12.05 pm. This train as already mentioned was notable for having the first half of the only scheduled working for the Southern Region's only BR Standard triple restaurant car set. In 1964 24-hour timetable its time was amended to 11.45 arriving at 17.23.

The 12.15 pm Portsmouth-Ilfracombe arriving at 5.56 pm was introduced in 1950, remarkable for being worked into North Devon by a light Pacific from Nine Elms. In 1957 it became an all-stations train reaching Ilfracombe at 6.05 pm. This was followed by the 10.50 am from Wolverhampton Low Level at 6.16 pm. This was changed to 6.35 pm in 1957 but disappeared from the timetable in 1964. The last trains of the day were the 6.05 pm Barnstaple Junction arriving at 6.48 pm; the 12.50 pm (later 1.00 pm) Waterloo at 7.18 pm; 4.35 pm Taunton at 7.37 pm; 2.50 pm (later 3.00 pm) Waterloo at 8.56 pm and finally the 8.28 pm Barnstaple Junction at 9.15 pm in 1949 only.

On Sundays the first train was the 10.45 am Barnstaple Junction Ilfracombe arriving at 11.26 am introduced in 1949. The 10.16 pm from Exeter came in at 12.48 pm (12.21 pm from 1957). The North Devon portion of the 9.00 am Waterloo introduced in 1959 arrived at 3.09 pm followed by the 10.45 am at 3.56 pm, introduced in 1953. In winter the 11.00 am from

Waterloo reached Ilfracombe at 5.06 pm but in summer its time varied from 10.35 am arriving at 4.04 pm in 1948 to 11.05 am arriving at 5.22 pm from 1955. The "Devon Belle" was next at 5.33 pm until 1954 and the last three trains of the day were the 5.10 pm Barnstaple Junction at 5.54 pm, the 1.54 pm Salisbury at 7.25 pm and the 4.00 pm Waterloo at 10.33 pm (10.48 pm until 1952). In 1964 all Sunday workings started from Exeter, at 11.55 am, 3.05 pm, 5.22 pm, 6.32 pm and 10.30 pm.

On weekdays the first train in the up direction was the 6.50 am to Barnstaple Junction which commenced running in 1955 and was extended to Kings Nympton (formerly South Molton Road) in 1957. The next service was to Waterloo at 8.10 am and the 9.00 am to Salisbury. The "Atlantic Coast Express" followed at 10.15 am (changed to 10.30 am in 1949) while on certain days up to 1954 the "Devon Belle" all-Pullman train left at 12.00 noon. There were then three trains to Waterloo at 12.15 pm (12.20 pm from 1949), 2.05 pm (later 2.20 pm) and 3.00 pm. The 4.45 pm to Exeter, 5.45 pm to Barnstaple Junction and 7.45 pm Exeter followed and the last train of the day was the 8.45 pm (8.30 pm from 1949) to Barnstaple Junction.

Up workings on summer Saturdays commenced with the 6.42 am to Barnstaple Junction introduced in 1955 and extended to Kings Nympton in 1957. This was followed by the 7.45 am to Taunton which became the 8.25 am to Manchester Exchange in 1953 and disappeared in 1964. The 8.10 am and 9.00 am to Waterloo came next and then the 9.25 am to Cardiff (9.20 am to Taunton from 1962). The Mortehoe-Waterloo train left at 10.00 am, at one time 9.40 am empty stock from Ilfracombe and later coming from Barnstaple Junction as the 8.00 am service train. The 10.15 am (10.30 am from 1953) to Waterloo was followed by a Taunton train at 10.25 am. This became the 10.12 am to Wolverhampton Low Level in 1958 and then the 10.10 am to Cardiff in 1962. The 10.55 am to Birmingham, Snow Hill, introduced in 1953 was extended to Wolverhampton Low Level the following year and retimed to 11.05 am in 1962. Two Waterloo trains left at 11.30 am and 12.00 noon, the latter originally being the "Devon Belle". A 12.35 pm to Waterloo ran until 1954. Replaced by a 12.25 pm to Paddington in 1956 it was cut back to Taunton in 1962. Waterloo trains left at 1.45 pm (until 1962), 2.10 pm and the last at 3.00 pm. The final trains of the day consisted of two to Exeter at 4.48 pm and 7.45 pm; three to Taunton at 5.15 pm, 6.50 pm (later 6.30 pm) and 8.10 pm and two to Barnstaple Junction at 5.45 pm and 8.30 pm.

On summer Sundays the first train was the 9.05 am to Exeter followed by the 9.50 am to Waterloo (10.30 am from 1959). This train was the return working of the SR triplicate restaurant car set referred to earlier. The 12.00 noon "Devon Belle" ran until 1954 followed by the 1.45 pm and 2.45 pm to

The Great Western through service to Ilfracombe (*Bradshaw*, October 1911).

LSWR passenger timetable for July 1914.

THE BARNSTAPLE AND ILFRACOMBE RAILWAY

Bradshaw July 1922 Passenger Timetable.

World War to their acceptance throughout, returned on summer Saturdays at the end of the through working of this train. Three through services ran from Paddington at 9.00 am, 1.40 pm and 3.30 pm. On Fridays there were two additional services from London: at 12.05 pm from Paddington and 6.00 pm from Waterloo. The fifteen up trains included four to Waterloo and two to Paddington. The service from Ilfracombe to Mortehoe and back continued to run. On Saturdays the twenty-four down trains included eight from Waterloo and six from Paddington, one of each being overnight. There was also a through train from Wolverhampton Low Level at 10.40 am. The 25 up services included eight to Waterloo, three to Paddington and one each to Bristol and Manchester. Nine down and ten up trains ran on Sundays that summer but all were taken off for the winter.

During the summer of 1939 eighteen down and sixteen up trains were run on Mondays-Fridays plus the Ilfracombe-Mortehoe service. On Saturdays twenty-four trains ran each way while on Sundays nine down and eleven up were run – a considerable improvement on the service provided 25 years previously. On summer Saturdays there was often block-to-block working with even double-headed trains banked to Mortehoe. Times taken between Paddington or Waterloo and Ilfracombe were both 5 hours. Sunday trains were withdrawn during the Second World War.

In January 1947 eleven down and ten up trains ran on weekdays with four each way on Sundays and on 20th June the Pullman "Devon Belle" made its inaugural run. By the following year the basic service was in operation which continued to the end of steam working on the branch. In 1948 the first arrival at 7.55 am on Mondays-Fridays was the newspaper train, the 1.25 am from Waterloo. It received a considerable acceleration in 1954 when it was timed to leave London at 1.15 am and reach Ilfracombe at 6.50 am, a stopping train following it from Exeter at 5.21 am. From 1955 the newspaper train was not scheduled to stop at Exeter St David's, the only occasion that such an omission appeared in the timetable, at least in recent years. The next arrival at 8.46 am was the 8.00 am from Barnstaple Junction followed by two through trains from Yeovil Town which had left at 6.20 am and 7.40 am. From February 1950 when common-user engine working was introduced, each of these was in charge of an Exmouth Junction light Pacific throughout. The next train, the 8.00 am from Salisbury, reached Ilfracombe at 1.47 pm and was followed by the 9.00 am from Waterloo at 3.53 pm (later advanced to 3.40 pm). From 1961 this terminated at Barnstaple Junction as progressive speeding up of the following "Atlantic Coast Express" resulted in the latter catching it up. The 10.50 am ex-Waterloo (later 11.00 am) then reached the terminus at 4.36 pm in 1948. Later improvements to this train are dealt with separately.

A 4.15 pm Barnstaple Junction-Ilfracombe was added in 1962, but before this, the next arrival at 5.33 pm on certain days only was the 12.00 noon from Waterloo, the "Devon Belle", also detailed in later pages. Following this were two local trains from Barnstaple Junction at 5.15 pm and 6.05 pm, preceding the 12.50 pm (1.00 pm from 1950) Waterloo to Ilfracombe. This train's arrival time was 7.18 pm in 1948, but by 1962 it had been advanced to 7.06 pm. Similarly the time of the next arrival, the 2.50 pm (later 3.00 pm) from Waterloo, advanced over the years from 9.13 pm to 9.08 pm. For most of the time this was the last train of the day, but in 1949 only, an 8.28 pm local ran from Barnstaple and in 1961 the 6.00 pm from Waterloo was extended to Ilfracombe on Fridays during the summer.

A similar service to the above ran on winter Saturdays, but during the summer was considerably augmented. Two overnight trains ran from Waterloo, the first originally leaving London at 11.50 pm and arriving Ilfracombe at 6.08 am. From 1953 it left at 12.35 am reaching its destination at 6.34 am but from 1959 it was departing at 12.15 am and arriving in North Devon at 6.14 am. The second left at 1.35 am (advanced to 1.15 am in 1954) and arrived at Ilfracombe at 7.55 am (6.53 am from 1954). Both were followed by the 5.26 am local from Exeter which ran into Ilfracombe at 7.42 am.

An arrival from Taunton at 8.31 am (amended to 8.12 am in 1953) was followed by the 8.00 am Barnstaple Junction which terminated at Mortehoe from 1959 but both these trains had disappeared from the timetable by 1962. Two further trains from Taunton used the line next: the first arriving at 9.05 am and the second at 9.58 am; they were introduced in 1955 and

Barnstaple Junction 31st August, 1963: ex-GWR 2-6-0 No. 7326 heads the 09.20 Ilfracombe – Taunton while ex-GWR Pannier 0-6-0ST No. 4666 on the left acts as station pilot. *S. Derek*

Waterloo (amended to 4.30 pm in 1962). The day finished with trains to Exeter at 6.10 pm and 7.50 pm and the 9.10 pm to Barnstaple Junction. In 1964 the service was reduced to five trains at 9.55 am, 1.10 pm, 4.30 pm, 6.15 pm and 8.00 pm all to Exeter.

The summer Sunday service of 1964 was a prelude to the pattern of future services and when full dieselisation took place on 7th September that year, ten down trains were run to take advantage of the diesel multiple units which had been placed in service, through trains were run from Exmouth (two), Sidmouth and Honiton, while additionally there were two through trains from Salisbury, but no through coaches from Waterloo. In the up direction there were nine trains with through workings to Kingswear, Exmouth (two), Honiton, Budleigh Salterton and, from 24th May, 1965, Paddington. Trains were allowed about 37 minutes between Barnstaple Junction and Ilfracombe. The summer timetable for that year showed seventeen down trains on Saturdays including six from Taunton to Ilfracombe (one from Carmarthen, one from Wolverhampton Low Level and three from Paddington), while there were eighteen up trains including eight to Taunton (one to Cardiff, one to Wolverhampton Low Level, two to Paddington stopping to pick up only on the Ilfracombe branch, plus one other through working to Paddington). The most interesting of these was the 11.05 am Paddington to Ilfracombe and its return working at 10.45 am which ran via Castle Cary, Yeovil and Exeter Central. On Sundays six trains were run in each direction with one through train to Paddington via Exeter. From 6th October no Sunday trains were run on the branch.

In 1966 nine trains were run each day on weekdays, and from 23rd May to 23rd September one through working to and from Paddington via Exeter. On summer Saturdays fourteen down trains were run including three from Paddington and one from Wolverhampton Low Level, while in the up direction there were fifteen including two to Paddington and one to Wolverhampton, six trains were run on Sundays, including one through to and from Paddington.

The service was further reduced in 1967, only five trains running each way daily, increasing to eight on summer Saturdays including two to and from Paddington but the Wolverhampton train had been dropped and there was no summer Sunday service. In 1968 the weekday service was reduced still further to five each way including a through train from Paignton. On summer Saturdays there were seven down (including one through from Paignton and two from Paddington) and seven up (including two through to Paddington). A similar service was run in 1969 and 1970 except that on summer Saturdays only one through train ran to and from Paddington.

A Swindon 3-car Cross-Country dmu leaves for Ilfracombe *circa* 1967.   *D. Payne*

The 17.18 Exeter Central – Ilfracombe at Barnstaple Town station on 27th July 1968. It comprised two 3-car dmu's headed by a Pressed Steel motor brake second.   *R.A. Lumber*

Freight Services

The freight service varied little over the years, always being worked from Barnstaple Junction since the Exeter-Torrington line was considered to be the main service. In 1909 the down direction saw a 5.10 am mail and goods from the Junction followed by a 10.16 am which called at Stoney Bridge Gates and Heddon Mill signal box when required to put out stores. A conditional path was allowed for a goods train from Braunton at 12.10 pm and a regular working to Pottington at 4.00 pm. In the up direction there was a path for a goods to Braunton at 11.30 am, followed by the 1.50 pm which called at Duckpool Crossing when required to put out stores and finally the return working from Pottington at 4.35 pm.

The 1938 timetable showed a 6.54 am from Barnstaple Junction to Ilfracombe followed by another at 10.19 am. A path was provided for working to the Town at 11.32 am. In the up direction there were goods trains at 6.25 am and 2.45 pm. Between Barnstaple and Braunton there were special limits:

50 wagons if 10 ton brake van
60 wagons if Class B power locomotive
55 wagons if Class C power locomotive
45 wagons if Classes D-G power locomotives
39 wagons if Class H-F power locomotives
35 wagons if Class K power locomotive.

Station	Turntables (Length of Rail)		Cranes or runways to lift				Weighbridges				Highway vehicle docks	Water columns	
	Engine	Wagon	Outside		Inside		Truck			Cart		No.	Where situated
			Ht. of lift		Ht. of lift		Capa-city Tons	Lth. in ft.		Capa-city Tons			
	ft. ins.	ft. ins.	T. cwts.	ft. ins.	cwts.	ft. ins.							
OOLEFORD JUNCTION TO ILFRACOMBE.													
Copplestone	—	—	5 0	14 8	40	15 4	—	—		7 (D 3½)	—	2	Down and up platfms
Morchard Road	—	—	5 0	14 0	40	14 6	—	—		—	1	—	—
Lapford	—	—	—	—	—	—	—	—		—	1	—	—
Eggesford	—	14 3	7 10	25 0	40	15 3	—	—		—	1	—	—
South Molton Rd.	—	—	5 0	16 6	40	15 6	—	—		—	1	—	—
Portsmouth Arms	—	—	5 0	17 1	—	—	—	—		—	—	—	—
Umberleigh	—	—	—	—	40	14 0	—	—		—	1	—	—
Chapelton	—	—	10 0	15 9	—	—	—	—		—	—	—	—
Barnstaple Jct.	50 0	—	7 10	22 3	40	17 9	—	—		—	1	4	Down platform, loco siding, turntable road and down loop
Braunton	—	—	10 0*	25 0	40	12 6	—	—		—	1	4	Up platfm (2), down platfm, level crossing
Mortehoe	—	—	1 5	14 6	—	—	—	—		—	1	—	—
Ilfracombe	64 10	—	10 0	21 6	40	15 0	—	—		—	1	1	Loco depot

Accomodation and Equipment at Stations, from the Southern Railway Working Timetable Appendices (Western Section) 1934. *Southern Railway*

'N' class 2-6-0 No. 31837 ascending the 1 in 36 gradient out of Ilfracombe with an up freight train, 6th August, 1952. *R.E. Toop*

In 1954 there were trains at 6.38 am and 10.36 am from Barnstaple Junction to Ilfracombe and a 4.25 pm to Pottington on weekdays. Return workings were at 2.37 pm and 5.45 pm from Ilfracombe and 6.50 pm from Pottington. On Sundays there was a single working at 7.55 pm from Barnstaple Junction to Ilfracombe. 1963 saw an 11.30 am to Ilfracombe and 4.25 pm to Pottington with return workings at 3.14 pm and 6.50 pm respectively. There was also a path for a 7.00 pm Ilfracombe-Barnstaple Junction goods.

The heavy gradients made the working of freight trains difficult and on at least one occasion a coupling on a down goods broke near Foxhunters Inn; the train ran away backwards, catch points turning the wagons into a meadow before they could plunge through the gates at Heddon Mill level crossing.

At one period the daily goods train was split at Braunton and taken over the bank in two separate trains, the same procedure being adopted for the return trip from Ilfracombe. Latterly freight trains shunted in the yards en route both going and returning from Barnstaple in order to avoid taking unnecessary wagons up the gradient.

Chapter Nine

Prestige Trains

The "Atlantic Coast Express"

On 19th July, 1926 the 11.00 am Waterloo-West of England train was named the "Atlantic Coast Express". It was the most multi-portioned train in the country; at times no less than nine different sections were included in its formation. The train comprised the Ilfracombe portion consisting of two third class brakes and a composite coach between, together with composite brakes for Torrington, Padstow, Bude, Plymouth, Exmouth, Sidmouth, and stations between Salisbury and Seaton. In addition there was a restaurant car section detached at Exeter. Before the opening of the Westbury route which gave the GWR an edge to competition for traffic to Plymouth, the predecessor of the "Atlantic Coast Express" was considered to be a Plymouth train with a connection for Ilfracombe; but with the opening of the GWR cut-off the Ilfracombe section assumed the major importance.

Until 1939 the "Atlantic Coast Express" hauled by a 4-6-0 locomotive covered the 83.8 miles to Salisbury in 86 minutes. A Mogul headed the Ilfracombe and Torrington sections from Exeter Central to Barnstaple Junction, where the Torrington coach was detached and the through

'N' class 2-6-0 No. 1829 calls at Barnstaple Town with the up "Atlantic Coast Express".
A.E. Box

Barnstaple Junction 1st August, 1952: 'West Country' class No. 34002 *Salisbury* heads the down "Atlantic Coast Express" while 'M7' 0-4-4T No. 30252 is in charge of the single coach train to Bideford. *R.E. Toop*

Ilfracombe coach from the "Cornish Riviera Limited" attached. This latter coach had left Paddington at 10.30 am, been slipped at Taunton and worked forward on a stopping train. Ilfracombe was reached at 4.06 pm, a journey of 5 h 6 m for SR and 5 h 36 m for GWR passengers. In the height of the summer, traffic was so heavy that two daily train services were needed, the 10.35am to Ilfracombe (arrived 3.35 pm), Torrington, Bude and Padstow and the 11.00 am to Sidmouth, Exmouth, Plymouth, Seaton and Lyme Regis, the last two detached at Salisbury and worked forward on the following stopping service. On summer Saturdays the "Atlantic Coast Express" became eight complete restaurant car trains between 10.24 am and 12.05 pm, the 10.24 am and 10.35 am being the Ilfracombe portions.

In 1939 the up winter working of the "Atlantic Coast Express" took 5 h 19 m for the journey to Waterloo. By 1948 all eight through portions from and to Waterloo were back in operation. Overall times were still slower than pre-war, particularly the up train which took 5 h 50 m because of additional stops. In the down direction the generous allowance of 103 minutes from Waterloo for the 83.8 miles to Salisbury caused problems for drivers of the "Merchant Navy" class locomotives who had to spin out the time and this fact was particularly obvious when the train was worked by Stanier Pacific No. 46236 *City of Bradford*, "Royal Scot" No. 46154 *The Hussar*, and Gresley's 'AA' Pacifics during the locomotive exchanges of 1948. The "Atlantic Coast Express" was speeded up in the summer of 1952 making it faster than pre-war, Exeter being reached 7 minutes earlier at 2.05 pm and Ilfracombe at 4.11 pm. In October 1961 the service was further accelerated, Exeter being reached 14 minutes before the 1939 time, Ilfracombe arrival being 3.55 pm. Then one by one the through coaches were withdrawn until only the Ilfracombe, Plymouth and restaurant car sections were left. In 1963 the WR took over all the former SR territory west of Salisbury and as it was decided not to run through services west of Exeter by this route, the "Atlantic Coast Express" made its last run on 5th September, 1964, the final day of regular steam working from Exeter to Ilfracombe.

The "Devon Belle"

The "Devon Belle", an all-Pullman service, first ran on 20th June, 1947. It carried a special headboard lettered yellow on a red ground while on the sides of the smoke deflectors were red wings similarly lettered. The train was inaugurated at a time when the SR was short of ordinary rolling stock but sufficient Pullmans were available. The two original

'West Country' class No. 34017 *Ilfracombe* heads the down "Devon Belle" 1st August 1952.
R.E. Toop

twelve-car trains consisted of a four-coach Plymouth portion formed of third class Pullman vehicles Nos. 36, 55, 171 and first class *Iolanthe* in one set, the third class Nos. 33, 54, 208 and first class *Argus* in the other, and an eight-coach Ilfracombe portion one of which contained third class Nos. 35, 60, 61, 65 and first class cars *Cynthia, Minerva,* and *Penelope*; the other set consisting of thirds Nos. 27, 32, 34, 249 and firsts *Princess Elizabeth, Rosamund* and *Fingall*. Each train was completed by a 27-seat observation car at the rear. These observation cars were converted from third class vehicles Nos. 13 and 14 by the Pullman Car Co. at its Preston Park Works. Although the train normally consisted of six cars for Ilfracombe and 4 for Plymouth, at the height of the season it was increased to 14 cars at weekends, with ten through to Ilfracombe. Hauling a 545 ton train between Waterloo and Exeter was no mean task even for a 'Merchant Navy', especially over the banks west of Salisbury. At first the Plymouth portion was taken over by 'West Country'

'West Country' class No. 34001 *Exeter* heads the up "Devon Belle", 1952.   *N. Wellings*

No. 21C103 *Plymouth* and the North Devon section by No. 21C117 *Ilfracombe* at Exeter Central, but later, numerous other members of the class took over their duties.

The "Devon Belle" left Waterloo at 12.00 noon and travelled non-stop to Wilton 2 miles west of Salisbury where it was allowed 6 minutes to change engines. The train was divided at Exeter Central, the Ilfracombe portion stopping at Barnstaple Town, Braunton and Mortehoe, arriving at the terminus 5 h 33 m after leaving London. The up "Devon Belle" also left at 12.00 noon and as well as being hauled by a 'West Country' class Pacific usually had one in the rear for banking up to Mortehoe. It took 5 h 20 m for its trip to Waterloo. At first the "Belle" operated on Fridays-Mondays only, but in the summer of 1949 it ran five days a week each way from Thursday to Monday in the down direction and Friday to Tuesday in the up. It ran only for the period of the summer timetable which was from June to September. As it did not pay, the Plymouth section was not run in the summer of 1950, the four cars terminating at Exeter Central. Ilfracombe was reached in 5 h 27 m. For the 1952 season it was proposed to run it on Saturdays only, but in the event it ran down on Fridays, Saturdays and Sundays and up on Saturdays, Sundays and Mondays. A major change took place to the Friday down train in 1954. Leaving Waterloo at 4.40 pm it called at Salisbury and Axminster in addition to the normal stop at Sidmouth Junction, reaching Exeter Central at 7.56 pm and Ilfracombe at 9.48. Nevertheless traffic declined still further and the train was withdrawn at the end of that season.

Armoured Train

Following the evacuation of Dunkirk, it was believed that the beaches near the mouth of the Taw offered potential sites for a German invasion. To assist the defence of this area, Lt General H.R. Alexander decided to move Armoured Train F to Barnstaple from Ashford, where it had been patrolling the Ashford-Hastings-Lewes line. It left Kent on 25th July, 1940, the wagons travelling in a civilian train while the engine ran light via Salisbury and Exeter, the Royal Engineers' crew being assisted by SR pilotmen. The following day the train was re-assembled at Barnstaple Junction, a convenient centre for patrolling the line between Bideford and Braunton, the train's specific task being defence against tanks, ships and seaplanes.

The original proposal for using armoured trains in the Second World War had been put forward by Lt Colonel Alan Mount, Royal Engineers,

Chief Inspecting Officer of the Ministry of Transport. He outlined his ideas to William A. Stanier and Sir Nigel Gresley so they could work out the means of implementation, the final design being decided at a meeting held in the loco yard at King's Cross towards the end of May 1940. An LMS 20 ton locomotive coal wagon was brought as the possible basis for an armoured truck and was accepted for the purpose. This all steel vehicle had a 12 ft wheelbase and 21 ft long body. For a distance of 4 ft, the sides were to be lowered from five to three feet in order to provide a complete circle of fire for the six pounder, 6 cwt Hotchkiss Mark II gun. Originally used by the navy in 1885, this particular variant of the weapon had been introduced in 1917 as the main armament for a tank. At this stage of the Second World War, it would have been effective against a German tank or armoured car at anything up to 800 or 1000 yards.

In order to avoid using steel which was in short supply, Stanier, responsible for the armoured trains' rolling stock, proposed that a strengthening layer of concrete be applied to the coal truck's interior. When the War Office observed that a bullet striking the exterior could cause a piece of concrete to fly off and kill those inside, a revised plan was adopted. This used an outer skin of $\frac{3}{16}$ inch mild steel plate welded to the wagon's exterior framing, the intervening four inches being filled with concrete. A transverse partition of similar construction was inserted, dividing the wagon into two compartments: a section just under 9 ft in length containing the gun, and a main compartment 12 ft 3 in. long. The latter had the additional protection of ¼ inch mild steel plates fixed above the wagon sides and angled inwards at 30° from the vertical to deflect bullets or splinters. Each sloping plate had three loopholes for rifles and Bren light machine guns, each armoured wagon having three of the latter. When not in use, the slits could be closed by sliding steel shutters. One armoured wagon in each train was in wireless communication with headquarters. A steel guard protected each axle box, while the substitution of screw couplings for the three-link type, demanded 2½in. wooden packing between the wagon frame and buffer beam. As the gun end formed the leading part of the train, T-section guard irons projected down from the underframe at the outer end of the wagon to thrust any obstruction off the track. Four brackets were also fitted at this end allowing the necessary head or tail lamps to be displayed. Here a removable steel ladder gave access to the wagon's interior.

Motive power was provided by ex-LNER 'F4' class 2-4-2T No. 7077, built in April 1909 by the Great Eastern Railway to James Holden's modification of Thomas W. Worsdell's design, this engine being on loan to the War Department from June 1940 until March 1943. Re-numbered

Armoured train 'K', LNER No. 7573, in February 1944. *Author's collection*

7185 in 1946, it was scrapped April 1948. In 1947 a brass plate was fitted carrying the inscription: "LNER. During the war of 1939/45 this locomotive was armoured and hauled defence trains on the coast lines." Armouring consisted of external plating over the side tanks, the lower part of the bunker which also contained water and the pipe linking them under the footplate. Plates screened the Westinghouse pump, boiler feed pipes, whistle and safety valve. Sliding plates covered the spectacle spaces and side openings, separate upper and lower doors enabling the cab to be totally enclosed. When in that state, the driver could be given instructions by bell signal from the leading wagon, but this facility was never used. Armouring raised the weight of the engine from 53 tons 19 cwt to 59 tons 18 cwt.

Behind the bunker was coupled a non-armour plated ammunition van (it did not carry ammunition for the six pounder, this being carried in the armoured truck), followed by an armoured wagon, while at the chimney end was a supply wagon containing a water pump, re-railing ramps and sleeper packing. This truck was a standard LMS 10 ft wheelbase 3-plank wagon modified with protective plates to the axle boxes and having screw couplings. Leading the train was another armoured wagon containing a six pounder gun. Initially the train was painted in camouflage, but later repainted black.

No spare engine was provided, but boiler washout and repairs did not interfere with patrols. The armoured engine was maintained by SR staff at Barnstaple Junction shed, Royal Engineers carrying out oiling duties and taking on water and the War Department reimbursed the SR for maintenance, coal and water. The Tank Corps were continuously on guard duty at the shed and when the train was fully manned, it had a crew of about 31 comprising:

Royal Tank Corps:	1 officer, 1 full sergeant, 24 privates;
Royal Engineers:	1 Company Sergeant Major, 1 sergeant, 1 driver, 1 fireman, 1 guard

All were billeted at the Waverley Hotel, Joy Street, Barnstaple, and later found accommodation in an empty shop in High Street. During 1942 men in the Tank Corps were replaced by those of the Polish Armoured Corps, all the latter being officers, yet acting as gun crew and carrying out train guard duties and were billeted near Barnstaple Junction Station.

The armoured train ran to schedule which varied with the time of year, as patrols were never at night or during daylight hours, but always at dawn or dusk, the time invasion was most expected. Although the train normally ran Barnstaple-Bideford-Barnstaple-Braunton-Barnstaple, the route was sometimes reversed to fit in with SR trains. In 1940 the train made an experimental run to Ilfracombe accompanied by an SR inspector with the wagon brakes being pinned down for descent to the resort, this event taking place before the addition of the tender. On the return journey (after climbing for about a mile at 1 in 36), although the engine steamed well, the water level in the boiler fell almost to nil, so it was deemed sensible not to add Ilfracombe to the new itinerary.

From October 1941, the emphasis was switched to Eggesford (on the line to Exeter), in order to give the crew familiarity with a wider area of operation, while the route through Torrington to Okehampton and Yeoford was followed periodically, together with occasional longer runs to Exeter, Newton Abbot, Bude and Taunton, the latter reached via Dulverton.

Regulations for running armoured trains were drawn up in consultation with the Railway Executive Committee, allowing for three conditions:

Condition A: this required an armoured train to be operated as a stopping passenger train, observing all the rules and regulations of the company, though in actual fact it did not carry the standard passenger headcode, but three white headlamps on the buffer beam of the leading wagon, though these could be extinguished by the authority of the train commander. No brake van was required, but a red tail lamp had to be carried at all times and kept lit during the hours of darkness. In the event, Condition A was the only condition under which the armoured train worked.

Condition B: this concerned patrolling when enemy action was an immediate possibility. A special bell code would have been put into operation between signal boxes, an armoured train being given priority over all other trains. Should a military situation have demanded its return while in mid-section, it would have been permitted to return "wrong line" to the next crossover in the rear, keeping to a procedure specially laid down.

Condition C: this would come into force when military operations against the enemy were in progress. The line would have been taken over by the Army and all civilian traffic suspended.

The Army footplatemen were required to pass the SR's rules and regulations to the satisfaction of the district locomotive superintendent and until this was done, SR pilotmen had to accompany them. Although there was no brake van, the train was required to carry a guard – rated as a brakesman-shunter - who travelled in the rearmost armoured wagon. A Royal Engineers' warrant officer, or staff sergeant,

Barnstaple locomotive yard 1940/41: the Royal Tank Corps (black berets) and Royal Engineers (khaki hats) form the crew of Armoured Train 'F'. *Author's collection*

accompanied the train commander in the leading truck to advise him on all matters concerned with railway operations and regulations. He passed all instructions to the footplate crew by electric bell, the code being:

    1 ring – stop
    2 rings – move chimney first 3 rings – move bunker first
    4 rings – slower
    5 rings – faster
    6 rings – open cylinder cocks

This last signal was the outcome of a suggestion which appeared in July 1940. "On cold or misty mornings it will be possible under favourable conditions to use exhaust steam from the cylinder cocks to blind a position or cover a withdrawal. This should be practised."

In the late summer of 1940 the train was returning from an early morning patrol to Braunton and travelling at about 30 mph on a "clear road", when the crews of the engine and leading armoured wagon were horrified to see the signal protecting Duckpool Crossing (east of

Braunton) return to danger. The crossing keeper, oblivious of the train's approach, was opening the gates to let a lorry cross. Although the engine driver applied his brakes, it was not possible for him to stop within the distance of 250 yds, the locomotive being the only vehicle fitted with Westinghouse brakes. The leading armoured wagon demolished the gates and smashed into the lorry's cab, killing the driver, a local man named Stanley Perkins. At the inquest the locomotive crew were absolved from all blame. As a sequel to his report on the accident, Brigadier A.G. Kenchington of the Royal Armoured Corps, although recognising that the provision of an armoured pipe would cause problems, recommended the War Office to fit Westinghouse brakes throughout each armoured train.

The solution was to have an additional braked vehicle behind the bunker. The LMS had some redundant ex-Caledonian Railway high sided bogie tenders designed to carry 4600 gallons of water on a system with no water troughs. These tenders were prepared for armoured trains at the LMS St Rollox Works, Glasgow. The War Office specification was for 3400 gallons, it probably being deemed necessary to keep the tank partly empty in order to preserve acceptable axle loadings, the armour plating weighing some nine tons and even with the reduced volume of water, a tender weighed 59¾ tons. Besides adding plating round the tank's sides, modification included axle box protection similar to the other vehicles on the train and adding buffing and draw gear at its leading end. Conversion started in December 1940, the tender arriving at Barnstaple about three months later.

This tender offered the addition advantage of augmenting the locomotive's water supply, as in the event of an invasion, it would have been a pity to have had to break off an engagement with the enemy in order to refill the tanks. Another modification to the train was that after working for nearly a year, a grenade net was issued to fit over the armoured wagons each time they went on patrol. This ensured the safety of the occupants, the route passing under quite a few bridges from which it would have been easy to "lob" a grenade down onto the passing train.

By the spring of 1942 fears of the south west peninsula being invaded had receded to such an extent that the armoured train was moved to Tilbury. It left Barnstaple on 20th April, the train being hauled complete (the engine running dead), extra vehicles being added to accommodate personnel and baggage. It followed the main line to Woking and then travelled via Kew and Cricklewood to Tilbury. Scheduled time for the whole trip was 14 hours 55 minutes including ten stops.

Oh, for a Holiday in Ilfracombe!
A holiday near to Nature's heart.

ILFRACOMBE
= THE BEAUTIFUL =
DEVON SEASIDE RESORT

THIS LOVELY TOWN, with its far-famed magnificent coastline, with brilliant sunsets, acts as a magnet to those seeking change of air and rest. Situated on the Coast of Devon, tourists make Ilfracombe their centre, being within easy reach of famous Clovelly to the West and the Lorna Doone country to the East.

Ilfracombe, possessing a most equable climate, is most suitable also as a Winter Resort.

Extensive Promenade and Southern Slope Park.

Summer Season, Easter to October.

Municipal Orchestra plays daily Easter to end of Season.

18-hole Excellent Golf Course. Deep Sea Fishing.

Municipal Putting and Bowling Greens.

Concert Hall, Pavilion and Public Swimming Baths reconstructed.

Alexander Theatre, leading London and Provincial Companies during Season.

Open-air Bathing in Pools; and Open Sea Bathing at Rapparee Beach.

Char-a-banc Tours daily over Dartmoor, Clovelly, Lynton, and other beauty spots of Devon.

Messrs. P. & A. Campbell's Steamer Trips daily to South Wales and Devon Seaside Holiday Resorts.

For Views of Ilfracombe, see pages 312 and 313.

Take your Holiday early and avoid the August rush.

Express Trains, Paddington, 5 hrs. 30 mins.

Illustrated Guide by S. P. B. Mais : Secretary, Holidays, Council Offices.

Post 2d.

WHEN WRITING TO ADVERTISERS PLEASE MENTION "HOLIDAY HAUNTS"

A full-page advertisement taken from the 1935 GWR *Holiday Haunts.*

Chapter Ten

Accidents

On Friday 3rd August, 1880 the 8.25 pm passenger train from Barnstaple to Ilfracombe consisted of "Ilfracombe Goods" No. 282 at the head of 5 coaches heavily laden with passengers and a wagon loaded with bricks. About three-quarters of a mile beyond Barnstaple Quay station and just as a curve to the right had been rounded, the engine encountered a series of bumps and left the road. Driver Whitehorne, who had worked on the line since its opening, shut off steam while Fireman Davolls applied the brake, but before it stopped, the locomotive fell on to the embankment on the river side. Fortunately speed was 20 mph so it only ran 70 yds before overturning. The wagon of bricks situated immediately behind the engine prevented the locomotive from going down the embankment and held it lying on its side a few feet from the top, the truck itself turning over sideways on to the permanent way. Had the wagon not been "inside the engine" the coaches may well have fallen 15 to 20 ft to the foot of the embankment. The only damage to the coaches was that the front panels of the first compartment were stove in and one of the buffers broken. No passengers were injured, but the driver was pinned down by his coat under the cab and was only

A coach shunted through the end of Ilfracombe station, February 1925.

Author's collection

extricated with difficulty, fortunately uninjured, unlike the fireman who was thrown against the dome and badly scalded by escaping steam.

When the 9.15 pm from Ilfracombe arrived at the scene of the accident it discharged its passengers who walked to the Quay station and it took up the passengers for Ilfracombe. By the following morning the lines were cleared of obstructions and early on Sunday 15th August No. 282 was raised by a steam crane and taken to Exeter where it was found to have suffered very little damage.

The derailment was caused by stones being placed on the rails and several tell-tale heaps of crushed stone were found on the lines. Some fishermen who passed along the line before the train came said that no obstruction was seen but some boys were playing in the vicinity. The culprits were caught and thrashed by their fathers in front of the station master.

On Christmas Eve 1889 the 3.54 pm from Ilfracombe consisted of "Ilfracombe Goods" No. 394, one LSWR coach, a meat van and two GWR coaches. Opposite the Foxhunters Inn about four miles from Braunton and two miles from Mortehoe, the engine left the road. After travelling along the ballast for 120 yds it turned to the left and fortunately the carriage turned to the right thus tending to prevent the engine from falling down the embankment. The only passenger injured was hurt by a tin box falling on her head from the luggage rack.

About 4.15 pm Mr Heather, the superintendent of the North Devon line, received a telegram informing him that the train which had left Mortehoe at 4.05 had not arrived at Heddon Mill, but he soon heard from there that the fireman of the derailed train had run to that signal box. The breakdown gang did not use a special train but travelled from Barnstaple on the 4.47 pm. At the scene of the mishap they cleared the down line by shifting slightly one of the coaches and the 4.47 arrived at Ilfracombe only about an hour late. A back-up breakdown crew of 16 men arrived from Exeter and by midnight the engine and coaches were re-railed. In the meantime, passengers in the through GWR coaches on the derailed 3.54 missed their connection, but the GWR ran a special train over the D&S to accommodate them.

One theory explaining the cause of the accident is that Lucas & Aird's men who were engaged in shovelling ballast in a quarry towards the doubling of the line, accidentally got stone on the "high" rail of the curve and caused the engine to be derailed instead of following the curve. The engine would have been lifted up so that the flanges were clear of the rail and then as it was on a curve it would have proceeded straight instead of following the curve and thus be derailed.

The Board of Trade inspector believed the cause to be excessive speed on the curve which must have been tempting to the driver as it was on a down gradient of 1 in 46. The inspector advised the use of four-coupled engines on all the Ilfracombe line passenger trains, or the easing of the gauge on the curves should the use of six-coupled engines be continued.

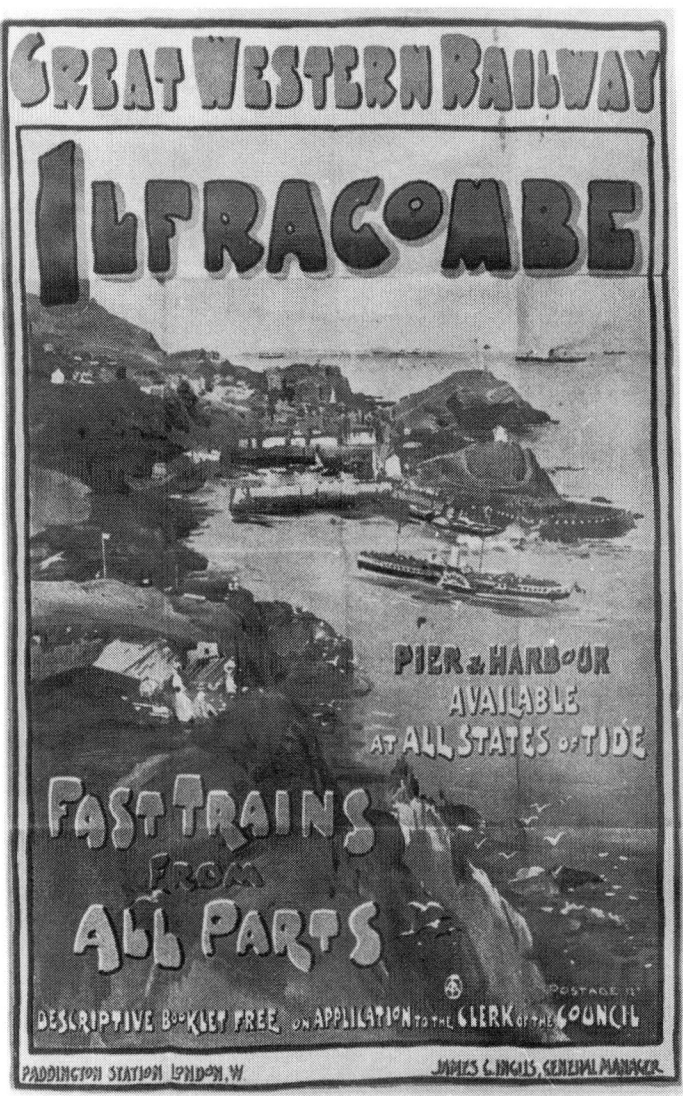

GWR advertising poster, January 1908.

British Railways Board

PUBLIC NOTICE — TRANSPORT ACT 1962

Withdrawal of Railway Passenger Service

BARNSTAPLE JUNCTION–ILFRACOMBE

The Western Region of British Railways hereby give notice in accordance with Section. 56 (7) of the Transport Act, 1962, that they propose to discontinue all railway passenger services between Barnstaple Junction and Ilfracombe and from the following stations:—

BARNSTAPLE TOWN, WRAFTON, BRAUNTON, MORTEHOE AND WOOLACOMBE, ILFRACOMBE

It appears to the Board that the following alternative services will be available:—

EXISTING SERVICES BY RAIL.

Barnstaple Junction station will continue to be served by the existing services.

EXISTING SERVICES BY ROAD

The Southern National Omnibus Co., Ltd.

SERVICE No.	ROUTE
101	Ilfracombe — Mullacott Cross (for Mortehoe and Woolacombe) — Braunton — Wrafton — Barnstaple (Southern National Office) — Barnstaple Junction Station — Bideford — Westward Ho!
102	Ilfracombe — Bittadon — Milltown — Muddiford — Barnstaple (Southern National Office).
103	Ilfracombe — Mullacott Cross — Mortehoe and Woolacombe Station — Woolacombe
108	Barnstaple (Southern National Office) — Wrafton — Braunton — Georgeham.

Any user of the rail service which it is proposed to discontinue and anybody representing such users may lodge an objection in writing within six weeks of 18th May, 1968, i.e., not later than 29th June, 1968, addressing the objection to —

The Secretary,
Transport Users' Consultative Committee
for the South Western Area,
Magnet House, 32, Victoria Street,
BRISTOL, L

If any such objection is lodged, the service cannot be discontinued until the Transport Users' Consultative Committee has considered the objections and reported to the Minister of Transport and the Minister has given his consent to the closure under Section 56 (8) of the Transport Act, 1962.

The Committee may hold a meeting to hear objections. Such a meeting will be held in public and any persons who have lodged an objection in writing may also make oral representations to the Committee.

If no objections are lodged to the proposal, the service will be discontinued on Monday, 7th October, 1968.

PADDINGTON STATION W 2.
MAY 1968.

L. W. IBBOTSON,
GENERAL MANAGER.

Closure notice in *Western Morning News* 9th May, 1968.

Chapter Eleven

Closure

With the increasing development of road transport, the line became uneconomic to operate. Summer traffic was still heavy, often block to block working being experienced and double-headed trains banked on the gradients, up to 10,000 passengers using the branch's stations on a summer Saturday, 5,470 passengers arriving at Ilfracombe on 27th July, 1957; but traffic outside the holiday season tended to be light. The branch was transferred from the Southern to Western Region on 1st January, 1963. All stations together with Rolle Quay Siding, Barnstaple, were closed to goods traffic on 7th September, 1964 when diesel multiple-unit working began, the last day of steam working being 5th September. The former D&S line closed on 3rd October, 1966, this further reducing the potential number of passengers able to use the Barnstaple to Ilfracombe section. As an economy measure the line was singled on 17th December, 1967. In 1967 1,603 passengers used branch stations on an average summer Saturday and 318 on an average summer weekday. At Ilfracombe 460 entrained and 589 alighted on an average summer Saturday. In 1968, as stocks of printed tickets ran out,

'Warship' class diesel hydraulic No, D820 *Grenville* at Mortehoe with the 11.10 Ilfracombe – Paddington 27th July, 1968. As an economy measure, the up line has been lifted recently. The young lady near the signal box is wearing an early example of a mini skirt.

R.A. Lumber

clerks filled in blank tickets by hand. The reason for this was revealed on 30th September, 1968 when the Exeter to Ilfracombe service was converted to conductor/guard operation, allowing closure of all booking offices north of Barnstaple Junction, including Ilfracombe. The guards issued tickets to every station in Devon, also principal stations to Bristol and London, other passengers having the trouble of re-booking at Exeter. On the same date, parcel facilities were withdrawn from Wrafton and Mortehoe & Woolacombe. In 1969 the Exeter-Barnstaple line was given a government grant of £174,000, but not the Barnstaple-Ilfracombe section. Closure of the line was announced by the Minister of Transport on 31st December, 1969, the money for an annual grant of £93,300 to keep the line open not being available. Costs were estimated as follows: track and signalling £56,400; terminals £23,400; movement £13,500; revenue only bringing in £13,300. Unfortunately there were eleven level crossings which needed manning and all added to the cost. It was suggested that the line be kept open for the summer months only, but this would not have greatly reduced annual expenses. The figure of £93,300 was criticised as being rather high when compared with the loss of £50,000 in 1964 and the fact that in the interim years track was singled, signal boxes closed and stations unstaffed.

The line closed on 5th October, 1970, the last train being the 7.55 pm from Ilfracombe on 3rd October consisting of an eight-car diesel multiple unit carrying about 500 passengers. On 26th February, 1975 an engineering inspector's saloon hauled by a Class 25 diesel locomotive traversed the branch to determine its condition but the rails were lifted later that year.

Industrial Dismantling Steel & Plant Limited of Exeter were let the contract for stripping down the iron bridge at Barnstaple and this proved almost as much trouble as erecting it, for thick black river mud washed down by the winter floods early in 1977 prevented the demolition men from working on the river bed at low tide. They were forced to wait until the summer when the sand was once more uncovered, access to the river bed being essential.

The Future

The North Devon Railway Society was formed in 1971 to re-open the line and from it (but as a quite distinct and separate body) the North Devon Railway Company Limited was formed in 1973 to negotiate, purchase and operate the railway, British Railways offering to sell the line and 142 acres for £410,000, the price rising later to £750,000. BR Standard Class 4MT 2-6-4 tank engine No. 80136 was reserved in the scrapyard at Barry, and a diesel service was envisaged for commuters between Braunton and Barnstaple. From 20th July until 28th September, 1974 a capital of £750,000 was on offer in 10p ordinary shares. About £20,000 was raised and following the death of the Acting Chairman of the company in December 1974, the Department of Trade & Industry was called in by a solicitor representing the remaining Directors to investigate the financial position.

More recently, in 2015, a group named Combe Rail was set up to preserve the heritage of the Barnstaple and Ilfracombe Railway. They are working on two main projects.

The first involves the section of the National Cycle Network from Ilfracombe to Willingcott, which uses the line of the old railway. In Ilfracombe they have negotiated with Pall Europe, who own the site of the former station, to restore its original pedestrian access and connect it to the cycle path. Along the cycle route they intend to place interpretation boards to inform path users about the history of the railway and its features. They are also seeking to restore the remaining railway infrastructure, of signal posts, platelayer's huts and gradient posts.

Their second project involves establishing a community light rail link along the River Taw from Braunton to Barnstaple station. It will run tram-like along the streets for parts of its route and utilise the line of the former railway where it can. It will require a new bridge over the River Taw, which will probably be parallel to Long Bridge. There is no mention in the plans about continuing the line from Braunton to Ilfracombe. However, if the line from Braunton to Barnstaple is built then proposals to continue it to Ilfracombe may follow.

BRITISH RAILWAYS
THE RAILWAY EXECUTIVE
WESTERN REGION

Telephone PASSENGER 3162
GOODS 3060

Station for CHELFHAM, BRATTON FLEMING, BLACKMOOR, PARRACOMBE, WOODY BAY, LYNTON and LYNMOUTH.

STATION MASTER
BARNSTAPLE JUNCTION

Your reference :—

Please quote this reference :—

Barnstaple Junction station master's letterhead.

AREAS 7, 7A, 11, 13, 13A

HOLIDAY RUNABOUT TICKETS
A WEEK'S UNLIMITED TRAVEL

During 1959 Holiday Runabout Tickets will be issued from 26th April to 31st October. They can be obtained at any station shown on the maps of this handbill and are valid for seven days from date of issue.

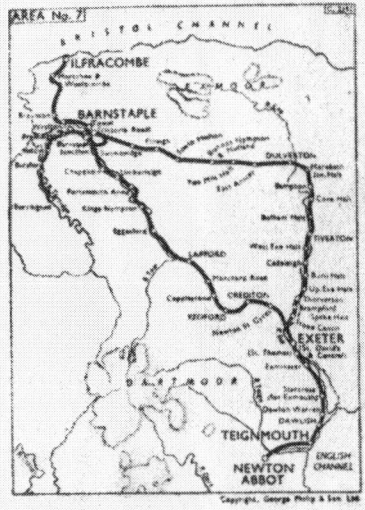 

JOINT AREA No. 7
Ilfracombe, Barnstaple, Torrington, Dulverton, Exeter, Newton Abbot.

AREA No. 13
Ilfracombe, Barnstaple, Okehampton, Exeter, Exmouth.

EACH AREA
18/6
SECOND CLASS ONLY

Tickets are also issued in conjunction with the above areas, permitting trips on Messrs. P. & A. Campbell's Bristol Channel Steamers from Ilfracombe to Lundy Island. Combined charge for each Area (7A and 13A) 31/- 2nd Class.

Passengers should enquire at stations for information regarding dates and times of steamer sailings (weather and circumstances permitting).

CHILDREN 3 YEARS AND UNDER 14 HALF-FARE
Holiday Runabout Tickets are not available by "CORNISH RIVIERA" Express trains, nor on Road Motors or on the Exmouth & Starcross Ferry.

For Area 11 and other charges see overleaf

Holiday Roundabout ticket handbill, 1959.

Appendix One

LSWR Working Timetable August 1874

Barnstaple and Ilfracombe line.
Speed must never exceed 25 miles per hour.
No engines except those specially constructed to work on Light Railways can be admitted on to the Ilfracombe line.
Very great care and caution must be used in working over the inclines.

Down

Miles		am	pm	pm	pm	pm
	Barnstaple Junction	8.57	12.08	3.34	5.50	8.35
½	Barnstaple Quay	9.04	12.15	3.41	5.57	8.42
5	Wrafton	9.17	12.28	3.54	—	—
5¾	Braunton	9.22	12.33	3.59	6.12	8.57
11¾	Mortehoe	9.42	12.53	4.19	6.33	9.18
14¾	Ilfracombe	9.52	1.03	4.29	6.43	9.28

Up

Miles		am	pm	pm	pm	pm
	Ilfracombe	6.35	10.10	2.00	4.45	7.20
3	Mortehoe	6.47	10.21	2.12	4.57	7.32
9	Braunton	7.05	10.38	2.30	5.15	7.50
9¾	Wrafton	7.09	—	2.35	—	7.54
14¼	Barnstaple Quay	7.23	10.54	2.48	5.32	8.08
14¾	Barnstaple Junction	7.30	11.00	2.54	5.39	8.15

Trains between Barnstaple Junction and Braunton and Ilfracombe will be worked under the Staff and Ticket System as well as Absolute Single Line Block Regulations.

Ilfracombe, view up May 1970; note the rising gradient. A 'Warship' clas diesel hydraulic heads the train. *S. Apperley*

Appendix Two

At first the line was subject to the Light Railways overall restriction of 25 mph and all trains approaching Ilfracombe were required to reduce speed to 4 mph for a quarter of a mile before the buffers, not a surprising restriction when it is remembered that the trains relied only on handbrakes.

Bulleid Pacifics were restricted to:
    55 mph Barnstaple Junction-Braunton
    40 mph Braunton-Mortehoe
    30 mph Mortehoe-Ilfracombe.

1969 speed limits were:
    15 mph Barnstaple Junction-Pottington signal box
    40 mph Pottington-Milepost 213 (1 mile beyond Barnstaple Town)
    55 mph Milepost 213-Braunton
    40 mph Braunton-Mortehoe & Woolacombe
    30 mph Mortehoe & Woolacombe-Ilfracombe
    (The same restrictions applied in the up direction.)

The last train before closure on 29th September 1935, of the Lynton and Barnstaple narrow gauge railway, about to leave Barnstaple Town. *Author's collection*

Appendix Three

Atlantic Coast Express Timings: 1936

Distance m.ch.		Time due a.m.	Schedule mins.	July 6th, 1936. 12 coaches, 387 tons "Lord St. Vincent". No. 856, 4—6—0 m. s.		August 11th, 1936. 11 coaches, 355 tons "Sir Aglovale". No. 781, 4—6—0 m. s.	
— —	WATERLOO dep.	10.35	—	— —	[10.35.18]	— —	[10.36.37]
3 71	Clapham Jct.		7	7 35	} signals	7 18	} very slight
12 02	Surbiton			18 11		16 36	} signals
19 10	Weybridge			25 54		23 18	
24 29	WOKING			31 8		28 18	
24 61	*Woking Jct. Box*		28	31 36		28 46	
33 20	Farnborough			40 01	} signals	38 11	} signals
39 70	Winchfield			49 20		45 7	
47 67	BASINGSTOKE			57 16		52 44	
50 26	*Worting Jct. Box*		54	60 5		55 22	
55 50	Overton			65 53		60 44	
61 11	Hurstbourne			70 39		65 20	
66 33	ANDOVER JCT.			74 47		69 18	
72 63	Grateley			80 30		74 46	
78 23	Porton			86 6		80 3	
82 52	*Tunnel Jct. Box*	p.m.	83½	89 50		83 37	
83 60	SALISBURY arr.	12.1	86	92 2	[12.7.20]	86 3	[12.2.40]
				No. 452, 4—6—0 "Sir Meliagrance". 12 coaches, 387 tons		No. 452, 4—6—0 "Sir Meliagrance". 11 coaches, 355 tons	
— —	SALISBURY dep.	12.6	—	— —	[12.12.39]	— —	[12.7.31]
2 41	Wilton			6 30		6 14	
17 48	Semley			23 41		23 50	
28 35	TEMPLECOMBE			33 5		33 53	
34 42	Sherborne			39 15		40 14	
39 09	YEOVIL JCT.		43	42 55		44 0	
47 73	Crewkerne			51 13		52 25	
55 77	Chard Jct.			59 25		60 52	
61 05	Axminster			63 12		65 8	
64 25	Seaton Jct.			65 45		67 55	
— —	152¼ m.p.			73 23		76 17	
73 66	SIDMOUTH JCT.			80 51		83 56	
83 20	Broad Clyst			86 45	} p.w.s.	90 8	
86 72	*Exmouth Jct. Box*		93	92 3		93 29	
89 00	EXETER CTL. arr.	1.42	96	94 20	[1.46.59]	95 36	[1.43.7]
				No. 1830, 2—6—0 6 coaches, 192 tons to Barnstaple Jct., 128 tons thence		No. 1496, 2—6—0 5 coaches, 160 tons to Barnstaple Jct., 96 tons thence.	
— —	EXETER CTL. dep.	1.47	—	— —	[1.51.48]	— —	[1.48.30]
0 55	,, St. David's a.			3	2 18	2 31	
— —	,, ,, d.			5	4 47	5 8	
12 18	*Coleford Jct. Box*			22	20 58	22 23	
28 75	Portsmouth Arms			46	43 36	44 52	signals
39 63	BARNST'PLE Jc. a.	2.47	60	56 55	[2.48.43]	59 46	[2.48.16]
— —	,, ,, d.	2.52	65	62 10	[2.53.58]	65 20	[2.53.50]
40 39	,, TOWN a.			68	64 32	67 41	
— —	,, ,, d.			69	65 29	68 49	
45 59	Braunton a.			77	73 36	76 49	
— —	,, ,, d.			78	75 36	77 55	
51 49	Mortehoe a.			95	92 25	91 30	
— —	,, ,, d.			97	93 30	93 20	
54 59	ILFRACOMBE a.	3.32	105	100 50	[3.32.38]	100 20	[3.28.50]

Appendix Four

Train Logs: 1932 and 1933

DOWN TABLE.

BRAUNTON TO MORTEHOE. 5 Miles 70 Chains.

ONE ENGINE.

Run No.	1		2		3		4	
Engine & Class	1830 N		1406 N		1406 N		1406 N	
Load, Tons Tare	91		32		112		96	
	m. s.	m.p.h.	m. s.	m.p.h.	m. s.	m.p.h.	m. s.	m.p.h.
BRAUNTON	0 00	—	0 00	—	0 00	—	0 00	—
218¾ m.p.	—	—	3 05	40·5	3 33	34·9	3 33	38·8
219¼ m.p.	5 01	—	4 30	42·9	5 13	36·3	4 58	44·1
220 m.p.	6 59	27·3	6 20	28·1	7 32	23·9	6 46	29·6
221¼ m.p.	7 59	32·1	7 27	27·9	8 37	28·8	7 44	31·7
221½ m.p.	9 03	28·1	8 41	25·0	9 46	25·8	8 51	25·7
222¼ m.p.	11 10	27·3	11 08	22·7	12 15	22·2	11 56	16·8
MORTEHOE	12 13	—	12 24	—	13 34	—	13 35	—

Run No.	5		6		7		8	
Engine & Class	1407 N		36 M7		1407 N		367 T1	
Load, Tons Tare	144		61		140		110	
	m. s.	m.p.h.	m. s.	m.p.h.	m. s.	m.p.h.	m. s.	m.p.h.
BRAUNTON	0 00	—	0 00	—	0 00	—	0 00	—
218¾ m.p.	3 49	34·9	3 51	32·3	3 35	36·3	—	—
219¼ m.p.	5 28	36·6	5 43	31·5	5 11	37·5	—	—
220¾ m.p.	7 57	19·7	8 36	18·8	8 12	14·9	9 00	17·3
221 m.p.	9 18	23·8	9 50	26·1	9 39	23·3	10 22	22·5
221½ m.p.	10 43	21·1	11 09	22·6	11 06	20·1	11 52	20·0
222¼ m.p.	13 27	23·4	14 16	17·7	14 20	17·5	15 08	17·6
MORTEHOE	14 38	—	15 39	—	15 43	—	16 27	—

TWO ENGINES.

Run No.	9		10		11		12	
Engines & Classes	34 M7		1836 N		1400 N		856 M7	
	— M7		250 M7		1828 N		377 M7	
Load, Tons Tare	144		138		192		206	
	m. s.	m.p.h.	m. s.	m.p.h.	m. s.	m.p.h.	m. s.	m.p.h.
BRAUNTON	0 00	—	0 00	—	0 00	—	0 00	—
218¾ m.p.	3 33	36·0	—	—	3 55	32·1	4 12	32·5
219¼ m.p.	5 09	37·5	5 14	—	5 49	30·0	6 03	31·9
220½ m.p.	7 37	20·5	7 38	20·9	8 46	18·8	9 05	17·7
221¼ m.p.	8 52	25·7	8 52	25·7	10 02	25·0	10 21	24·4
221½ m.p.	10 11	22·5	10 15	20·9	11 20	22·5	11 48	19·8
222¼ m.p.	13 02	19·2	13 08	20·5	14 04	20·5	15 04	18·7
MORTEHOE	14 30	—	14 34	—	15 28	—	16 08	—

THREE ENGINES.

Run No.	13		14		15		16	
Engines & Classes	1832 N		1841 N		376 M7		1831 N	
	242 M7		250 M7		1840 N		2696 E1/R	
	34 M7		256 M7		669 M7		376 M7	
Load, Tons Tare	360		354		355		325	
	m. s.	m.p.h.	m. s.	m.p.h.	m. s.	m.p.h.	m. s.	m.p.h.
BRAUNTON	0 00	—	0 00	—	0 00	—	0 00	—
218¾ m.p.	4 07	31·0	4 11	33·3	4 10	34·6	4 11	29·6
219¼ m.p.	5 58	32·8	5 53	36·0	5 53	34·6	6 14	27·8
220¾ m.p.	8 55	17·9	8 25	19·2	8 38	18·4	9 24	19·7
221¼ m.p.	10 14	24·8	9 50	22·0	9 56	23·7	10 35	25·8
221½ m.p.	11 37	21·4	11 25	18·6	11 26	19·6	11 54	22·2
222¼ m.p.	14 37	18·6	14 38	18·0	14 38	18·0	14 53	18·4
MORTEHOE	15 51	—	15 58	—	16 00	—	16 07	—

Note.—The speeds are calculated on the ¼-mile timings at the respective posts. Distances from Waterloo are: Braunton, 217m. 39ch.; Mortehoe, 223m. 29ch.; Ilfracombe, 226m. 39ch.

Train logs made by F.E. Box in 1932 and 1933

UP TABLE.

ILFRACOMBE TO MORTEHOE. 3 Miles 10 Chains.

ONE ENGINE.

Run No.	1		2		3		4	
Engine & Class	35 M7		1840 N		693 700		361 T1	
Load, Tons Tare	70		94		82		70	
	m. s.	m.p.h.	m. s.	m.p.h.	m. s.	m.p.h.	m. s.	m.p.h.
ILFRACOMBE	0 00	—	0 00	—	0 00	—	0 00	—
226 m.p.	0 50	—	0 53	—	1 18*	—	1 11	—
225½ m.p.	2 37	17·4	2 35	18·4	3 27	17·0	3 08	16·7
225 m.p.	4 01	22·5	4 06	20·0	4 55	21·4	4 44	20·0
224½ m.p.	5 24	22·3	5 47	18·0	6 25	20·0	6 20	20·0
224 m.p.	6 45	22·3	7 20	19·2	7 55	19·6	7 59	18·4
223½ m.p.	7 52	27·1	8 33	20·0	9 06	32·1	9 16	28·1
MORTEHOE	8 51	29·2	9 35	28·1	9 55	33·3	10 15	27·3

Run No.	5		6		7		8	
Engine & Class	1828 N		4313 G.W.R. 2-6-0		1832 N		1 T1	
Load, Tons Tare	145		87		150		100	
	m. s.	m.p.h.	m. s.	m.p.h.	m. s.	m.p.h.	m. s.	m.p.h.
ILFRACOMBE	0 00	—	0 00	—	0 00	—	0 00	—
226 m.p.	0 53	—	1 03	—	1 03	—	1 10	—
225½ m.p.	2 45	16·4	3 13	14·1	3 10	14·3	3 27	13·4
225 m.p.	4 31	17·0	5 08	16·1	5 08	15·5	5 31	15·3
224½ m.p.	6 20	17·0	6 56	17·0	7 09	15·8	7 32	16·6
224 m.p.	8 00	18·0	8 44	16·1	9 03	15·8	9 24	16·4
223½ m.p.	9 18	27·3	10 06	27·3	10 24	28·1	10 46	27·3
MORTEHOE	10 19	28·1	11 01	28·1	11 18	28·1	11 40	29·0

TWO ENGINES.

Run No.	9		10		11		12	
Engines & Classes	1840 N 1853 N		1408 N 376 M7		1832 N 36 M7		256 M7 375 M7	
Load, Tons Tare	100		91		102		169	
	m. s.	m.p.h.	m. s.	m.p.h.	m. s.	m.p.h.	m. s.	m.p.h.
ILFRACOMBE	0 00	—	0 00	—	0 00	—	0 00	—
226 m.p.	0 58	—	0 56	—	0 51	—	0 58	—
225½ m.p.	2 48	17·3	2 39	19·4	2 51	17·0	2 58	15·3
225 m.p.	4 13	22·5	4 03	22·0	4 20	20·5	4 32	20·0
224½ m.p.	5 38	21·4	5 33	20·2	5 54	20·0	6 05	19·6
224 m.p.	6 58	23·1	7 00	20·7	7 20	21·4	7 38	19·2
223½ m.p.	8 01	31·0	8 08	30·8	8 31	29·0	8 56	26·5
MORTEHOE	8 58	32·1	9 12	30·2	9 30	31·0	10 01	26·5

TWO ENGINES. THREE ENGINES

Run No.	13		14		15		16	
Engines & Classes	1843 N 1406 N		1854 N 1407 N		1846 N 242 M7		5569 G.W.R 2-6-2T 256 M7 1838 N	
Load, Tons Tare	258		272		258		254	
	m. s.	m.p.h.	m. s.	m.p.h.	m. s.	m.p.h.	m. s.	m.p.h.
ILFRACOMBE	0 00	—	0 00	—	0 00	—	0 00	—
226 m.p.	0 54	—	0 55	—	1 05*	—	0 55	—
225½ m.p.	3 01	16·3	3 11	14·4	3 20	14·0	3 19	13·6
225 m.p.	4 40	18·4	5 06	15·6	5 20	15·0	5 14	15·8
224½ m.p.	6 25	17·4	7 01	16·9	7 24	15·0	7 12	15·6
224 m.p.	8 03	18·4	8 47	16·7	9 22	15·2	9 07	15·3
223½ m.p.	9 18	28·3	10 09	26·6	10 48	25·3	10 40	24·7
MORTEHOE	10 14	30·8	11 21	26·6	11 52	26·5	11 52	26·8

*Engines slipped at start.

Appendix Five

Instructions affecting Western Region Staff when working over the SR: October 1960

BARNSTAPLE JUNCTION 'A' TO ILFRACOMBE.
BARNSTAPLE JUNCTION.

VEHICLE RESTRICTION.—Bogie stock with step boards between the bogies fitted at a height of less than two feet from rail level to the underside of the brackets supporting such step boards, other than S.R. bogie guards vans Nos. 201 to 280 inclusive and 350 to 399 inclusive, must not pass over the bridge between Barnstaple Junction and Barnstaple Town.

This restriction does not apply to vehicles with short step boards attached only to the bogies.

BRAUNTON—ILFRACOMBE.

PASSENGER TRAINS.—All trains between Braunton and Ilfracombe must have vehicles with a brake compartment as follows:—

Not exceeding 180 tons—1 bogie vehicle with a brake compartment. This vehicle to be included in the total tonnage and, in the case of vehicles conveying passengers from Braunton to Mortehoe & Woolacombe or Ilfracombe to Mortehoe & Woolacombe, it must be attached at the rear of such vehicles except when an assisting locomotive is provided in the rear.

Exceeding 180 tons.—2 bogie vehicles with brake compartments, 1 of these vehicles must be marshalled at the rear. These vehicles to be included in the total tonnage and the guard must travel in the rear brake vehicle.

Two horse boxes, cattle vans, carriage trucks, vans or similar vehicles fitted with the continuous brake complete and provided with a hand brake may be attached outside the rear vehicle with a brake compartment, but this number must not be exceeded.

Should the continuous brake become inoperative, the load must be reduced so that the train may be safely controlled on any part of the inclines with the hand brake power available.

ASSISTANCE ARRANGEMENTS.—The undermentioned instructions regarding the assistance of trains from Braunton to Mortehoe & Woolacombe and from Ilfracombe to Mortehoe & Woolacombe are supplementary to those appearing in Table 'J'. When the loads are within those specified for the class of locomotive concerned it may be necessary in certain conditions for an assisting engine to be provided and such assistance must be arranged at the request of the driver.

The maximum loads for passenger and coaching stock trains worked by one locomotive are as follows:—

Class	Tons
Braunton to Mortehoe & Woolacombe	
West Country & Battle of Britain	240
N.	180
U.	150
M.7	140
T.9	100
L.M.2 (2-6-2T)	140
W.R. 63xx	190
W.R. 45xx	150
W.R. 22xx	120
Ilfracombe to Mortehoe & Woolacombe	
West Country & Battle of Britain	205
N.	180
U.	150
M.7	140
T.9	100
L.M.2 (2-6-2T)	140
W.R. 63xx	180
W.R. 45xx	140
W.R. 22xx	110

Trains exceeding the weights shown must have an assisting engine which may be attached at the front provided the load does not exceed 280 tons. When this tonnage is exceeded the assisting engine must be attached at the rear. Trains must not consist of more than 88 wheels.

When a freight train requires assistance, the assisting engine must be attached in rear.

FREIGHT TRAINS—MORTEHOE & WOOLACOMBE TO BRAUNTON OR ILFRACOMBE.—
Trains must not exceed a load equal to 25 loaded wagons inclusive of brake van.

A train worked by one locomotive only must have brake vans attached, with a man in each, as follows:—

Load inclusive of brake van.	Brake van to be provided.
Not exceeding equal to 15 loaded wagons	1 heavy van.
Above 15 and not exceeding 25 loaded wagons	2 heavy vans.

When two brake vans are attached, one van must be placed at the rear of the train and the other behind the eleventh vehicle of the train.

A train worked by two locomotives must have both locomotives at the front and in such cases one brake van only need be provided.

The driver and guard will be held responsible for communicating with one another and observing the requirements of Rule 131 (ii) when circumstances indicate that the state of the rail would be unfavourable for the prompt stoppage of trains.

Should any fitted vehicles be attached, they must, as far as practicable, be marshalled next to the locomotive and the brake pipes connected, in which case they need not be included when calculating the number of brake vans required.

FITTED STONE TRAINS.—Such trains, fitted with the continuous brake throughout, must be operated in accordance with the instructions applicable to passenger trains, with the exception that the load must not exceed six loaded bogie hopper wagons and two fitted brake vans.

ILFRACOMBE.

SHUNTING.—Freight vehicles must not be hauled up the incline during shunting operations except in unavoidable cases when a brake van, in which the shunter must ride, must be attached at the station end.

The view from the rear window of an up Swindon 3-car Cross-Country dmu departing from Barnstaple Town station *circa* 1967.   *D. Payne*

Appendix Six

Station Statistics

	Ilfracombe Town Office		Ilfracombe Station	
	1930	1935	1930	1935
Passenger tickets	2,513	2,181	46,245	24,721
Season tickets	69	73	413	495
Platform tickets	—	—	16,697	11,993
Dog etc tickets	38	37	686	316
Excess fares	50	58	447	428
Tickets collected	—	—	125,717	99,609
Cloakroom tickets	—	—	2,443	11,924
Telegrams/tel. Calls	118	1,089	3,399	2,661
Parcels forwarded	733	1,159	5,681	4,131
Parcels received	—	—	66,884	53,192
Checked luggage	4,616	4,823	3,508	4,604
Milk cans forwarded			3	117
Milk cans received			1,599	10,724
Fish forwarded (cwt)			1,154	1,022
Fish received			3,962	3,952
Coaching vehicles loaded			41	3
Coaching vehicles unloaded			59	2
General merchandise forwarded (tons)			1,346	833
General merchandise received			7,705	6,328
Coal etc forwarded			1,919	1,242
Coal etc received			2,740	4,670
Other minerals forwarded			430	443
Other minerals received			3,912	2,284
Livestock forwarded			5	—
Livestock received			73	—
Loaded wagons forwarded			2,221	2,204
Loaded wagons received			4,356	3,966
Passenger receipts £	2,254	2,742	12,540	7,304
Season £	86	52	238	423
Parcels £	502	548	1,766	1,458
General merchandise £			4,736	2,753
Coal etc £			485	321
Other minerals £			873	362
Livestock £			61	—
Lavatory pence			7,416	4,459
Staff	3,019	3,343	19,291	11,862

Mortehoe		Braunton		Barnstaple Town	
1930	1935	1930	1935	1930	1935
17,798	12,208	45,096	22,117	71,711	51,494
113	84	110	124	411	451
722	143	28	—	6,376	3,284
330	187	503	212	974	549
111	188	436	288	610	502
43,440	30,173	59,224	33,003	141,819	110,699
180	201	1,273	189	2,444	2,429
787	857	1,444	1,045	866	465
1,422	1,181	6,010	4,884	6,967	6,291
6,422	7,438	9,818	12,354	412	629
650	1,142	1,623	1,161	80	198
—	7	—	1,011	5	180
90	389	219	843	1	—
44	97	4,508	6,405	2,274	1,634
746	411	176	105	486	15
15	11	161	239		
47	15	30	2		
272	183	1,122	1,001		
1,844	1,153	3,002	2,535		
4	—	—	—		
1,659	1,689	2,589	3,216		
12	71	384	655		
963	1,604	2,714	2,771		
133	211	10	169		
32	—	22	11		
79	95	298	601		
—	763	181	1,635	2,026	
2,829	1,795	4,065	3,207	7,741	4,131
119	170	83	127	108	167
462	456	2,366	2,426	849	520
293	210	2,122	1,923		
4	2	12			
74	252	672	817		
14	18	20	7		
1,728	1,596	720	432	8,032	3,538
3,701	2,681	7,031	8,370	8,819	4,873

Bibliography

Acts of Parliament
Titled Trains of Great Britain; C.J. Allen
The Southern Since 1948; G.F. Allen
Southern Country Stations, Vol. 1: LSWR; R. Antell
The Armoured Train; S. Balfour
BR Steam Motive Power Depots, SR; P. Bolger
Locomotives of the LSWR; D.L. Bradley
London & South Western Railway Locomotives, The Adams Classes; D.L. Bradley
London & South Western Railway Locomotives, The Drummond Classes; D.L. Bradley
Bradshaw's Manual 1869
Bradshaw's Railway Guides
Closed Stations and Goods Depots; C.R. Clinker
West Country Passenger Steamers; G. Farr
Engineering
Barnstaple; W.F. Gardiner
GWR Rule Book 1936
The North Devon Coast; C.G. Harper
Great Western Coaches from 1890; M. Harris
An Historical Survey of Southern Sheds; C. Hawkins & G. Reeve
Devon; W.G. Hoskins
Ilfracombe Railway Minute Books
The Centenary of the Barnstaple-Ilfracombe Line; J. Lock
Railways Round Exmoor; R. Madge
Southern Steam; O.S. Nock
Track Layout Diagrams of the Southern Railway and BR SR, Section S6; G.A. Pryer
Railway Magazine; particularly Vol. 9 p.177; Vol. 20 p.424; Vol. 45 p.408; Vol. 46 p.80
Railway Modeller 1970 pp.209 and 254
Railway World 1974 p.310
Railway World Annual 1975 p.128
Locomotives of the LNER, Part 7; RCTS
Main Lines to the West; S. Rocksborough-Smith
London & South Western Railway; G.A. Sekon
The London & South Western Railway, Vols 1 & 2; R.A. Williams

NEWSPAPERS: *Bristol Mercury; Bristol Times & Mirror; Express & Echo; Ilfracombe Chronicle; Ilfracombe Gazette; Ilfracombe Observer; North Devon Journal-Herald; Western Morning News*

FILM: An early film View from an Engine Front (National Film Archive) shot in 1898 shows part of a journey from Barnstaple Junction to Ilfracombe.

Index

Accidents 24 *et seq.*, 32 *et seq.*, 48, 50, 60, 79, 114 *et seq.*, 117 *et seq.*
Acts of Parliament 8, 10, 12 *et seq.*, 15 *et seq.*, 22 *et seq.*, 32, 67
Adams, W. 69, 71
Armoured train 109 *et seq.*
Atlantic Coast Express 77, 80 *et seq.*, 89, 97, 99, 105 *et seq.*, 127
Attwood & Co. 31
Avery, J. 12

Barnstaple 5, 7, 9, 11, 16 *et seq.*, 26 *et seq.*, 42 *et seq.*, 67 *et seq.*, 76, 80, 83 *et seq.*, 92 *et seq.*, 112 *et seq.*, 121 *et seq.*
Bartlett, J. 25
Beattie, J. 69
Beattie, W. G. 22, 69
Bickington 25
Bideford 5, 22, 31, 37, 113
Bircham & Co 9 *et seq.*, 12
Bishops Tawton 10, 12
Bittadon 9, 11, 22
Blizzard 34
Board of Trade 29
Brassey, T. 7 *et seq.*, 13
Braunton 9 *et seq.*, 12, 17, 19, 22 *et seq.*, 29 *et seq.*, 33 *et seq.*, 48, 50, 53, 73, 84, 89, 103 *et seq.*, 109, 113 *et seq.*, 123
BRIDGE
  Barnstaple 29 *et seq.*, 33, 42
  Swing 30, 33, 47 *et seq.*,
  Other 34, 50, 68
Briss, C. 25
Bristol & Exeter Railway 5, 7 *et seq.*, 12, 16
Bristol & Portishead Railway 5
Burlinson, N. J. 88

Cairn Top 25
Campshot 25
Carter, G. 13
Church, Mr 29
Clarke, F. 16
Coaches 29, 31, 33, 60, 65, 67 *et seq.*, 81 *et seq.*, 107 *et seq.*, 117 *et seq.*
Coaches, camping 50
Cobley, Seymour 53
Crediton 7
Crich, J. 25

Davolls, Fireman 117
Dean, C. 7
Devon & Somerset Railway 11, 13, 15 *et seq.*, 27, 67 *et seq.*, 87
Devon Belle 65, 81 *et seq.*, 97, 99 *et seq.*, 107 *et seq.*
Doubling track 33 *et seq.*, 50
Drummond, D. 79
Dutton, R. H. 15

Errington, J. E. 9, 11
Exeter 7, 93 *et seq.*, 105, 108 *et seq.*, 113, 118, 122
Exeter & Crediton Railway 37
Exmouth Railway 10, 16

Fell, J. B. 19
Fisher, Mr 28 *et seq.*
Fowler, J. 12 *et seq.*
Foxhunters Inn 10, 17, 25, 29, 33 *et seq.*, 104, 118
Fremington 19

Galbraith, W. R. 9 *et seq.*, 13, 16, 19 *et seq.*, 22, 24, 26, 29
Gauge 7, 10 *et seq.*, 15, 42
Georgeham 84
Gould, Mr 20
Gould, W. R. 23
Gradients 10 *et seq.*, 15, 17, 20, 29 *et seq.*, 53, 59, 69, 71, 73, 76, 83 *et seq.*, 104, 119, 121
Great Central Railway 93
Great Western Railway 12, 18, 30, 33, 39, 67, 79, 82, 88 *et seq.*, 105 *et seq.*, 118
Grierson, J. 67

Harbour 10 *et seq.*, 15 *et seq.*
Harrison, T. E. 12
Hartnoll, G. 24
Heanton Court 9, 50
Heather, Mr 34
Heddon Mill 53, 83 *et seq.*, 103 *et seq.*
Herepath, J. 7
Higgs, Mr 29
Hughes, Messrs 30
Hutchins, E. J. 15
Hutchings, J. 25
Hutchinson, Col, C. S. 29
Huxtable, R. 12
Huxtable, W. 12, 15

Ilfracombe 5 *et seq.*, 15 *et seq.*, 34 *et seq.*, 37, 39, 59 *et seq.*, 76, 80, 82 *et seq.*, 93 *et seq.*, 100 *et seq.*, 117, 121 *et seq.*

Jacomb, W. 28 *et seq.*
Jenkins, Mr 20

Kenchington, Brigadier 115
King, W. 24
Knowle 53

Landmann, Colonel 7
LOCOMOTIVES
  Gnat 25, 27
  Whitmore 28
  Ilfracombe Goods 28 *et seq.*, 31, 69, 71, 74
  Other 39, 60, 65, 69 *et seq.*, 103, 105 *et seq.*, 110 *et seq.*, 117, 121

London & South Western Railway   6 et seq., 15 et seq., 22 et seq., 27, 29, 30 et seq., 65, 67 et seq., 84, 88 et seq., 93
Lucas & Aird   32 et seq., 35, 118
Lucas & Wilkinson   19
Lynton   5 et seq.
Lynton & Barnstaple Railway   42, 47 et seq. 88

Mangles, C. E.   9, 15 et seq.
Mair, Mr   28
McConnel, M.   22
McMillen, J.   16
Maunsell, R. E. L.   71, 81
Midland Railway   5 et seq., 88
Ministry of Transport   60, 110, 122
Moon, R. H.   13
Moore, Rev. W. C.   23
Mortehoe   17, 24, 27 et seq., 50, 53, 55 et seq., 73, 83 et seq., 93 et seq., 100, 109, 121 et seq.

North Devon Railway & Docks   7 et seq., 22, 37
North Eastern Railway   12

OPENING
   Barnstaple   7 et seq.
   Barnstaple GWR Loop   67 et seq.
   Ilfracombe   28 et seq., 60

Paddington   87, 101
Pain, T.   23 et seq.
Palmer, Inspector   35
Perkins, S.   115
Permanent way   26, 35, 83 et seq., 118
Perry, Messrs   27
Pickering, Messrs   18
Pilton   24, 26, 48
Pottington   19, 27, 32, 34, 48, 50, 84, 103 et seq.
Price, Rev. B   8, 10, 12, 15, 19, 23
Pullman Car Co.   81, 97, 100, 107 et seq.

Raleigh Cabinet Works   42
Rice, Mr   32
Rolle, Mr   24
Rolle Quay   48, 50

Score   25
Scott, A.   17, 22, 29, 67
Sharp, R   13
Signalling   37 et seq., 42, 47 et seq., 50, 60, 65, 84 et seq.
Slade   10, 24, 58 et seq.
Slocombe, Mr   24
Smith, W. H.   60
South Eastern & Chatham Railway   71
South Molton   31
Southern Railway   50, 73, 82, 87, 93, 99, 112 et seq
Steamers   5
Stoneman, P.   23
Stoney Bridge   33, 53, 84, 103
Stuart, Vice-Chancellor   18

Taunton   11, 15, 79 et seq., 98 et seq., 106, 113
Tawstock   26, 28
Taylor, J.   23, 29
Tite, W.   9, 37
Toms W. S.   12 et seq., 15
Torrington   23, 31, 39, 74, 87, 103, 105, 113
Trench Colonel A. C.   60
Trimstone   19
Tunnel   11 et seq., 19, 25 et seq., 32 et seq., 59
Twitchen   19
Tyler, Mr   29

Vye, Captain   13

Waring, Messrs   13
West Down   19, 24, 34
Westacott, W.   22
Whitehorn, Driver   117
Whitley Mr   12
Williams, Sir William   9 et seq., 19, 22, 26
Willingcott   25
WORLD WAR
   First   79, 82, 93
   Second   93, 109 et seq.
Wrafton   9, 17, 50, 84, 87, 89, 122
Wreford, R.   7 et seq., 16, 24

Front cover: 'Battle of Britain' class Pacifics Nos. 34075 *264 Squadron* and No. 34069 *Hawkinge* climb past Upper Slade Reservoir with the 14.55 Ilfracombe to Waterloo express on the 27th July, 1963.   *P.W. Gray*

Back cover: Devon Belle poster, 1947.